Nutrition & Activity Program
for
Teen Girls

Betty Kern, MS, CSCS

Nutrition & Activity Program for Teen Girls
Copyright 2009 by Betty Kern, MS, CSCS
All rights reserved.

Published by:
Holy Macro Books
13386 Judy Ave. NW
Uniontown, Ohio, USA 44685

Contributing editor: Lisa Hostler

Illustrations by Betty Kern, MS, CSCS
ISBN# 978-932802-45-0

This book is dedicated to all of my wonderful girls at SHS who helped make this program possible! Thank you for working so hard, all of the laughs and occasional surprises...
I truly enjoyed teaching each one of you!

A special thanks to Mrs. Cynthia Frola, my principal, for believing in me and the "Personal Training Program!" Your love & support helped make it all possible!

About the author:

Mrs. Betty Kern teaches Physical Education and Math at Springfield High School in Akron, Ohio. Betty's Master's degree is in Exercise Physiology and Fitness. She is a Certified Strength & Conditioning Specialist through the National Strength & Conditioning Association. She has completed several levels of training with Yogafit and continues to advance her fitness repertoire through learning new group fitness activities.

It was Betty's desire to help the girls at Springfield high school make the connection between their physical activity & nutrition habits and their energy levels, physical fitness, school performance, weight and health issues. The Personal Training Class for girls was born out of this desire and proved to be extremely popular and successful at SHS! Betty developed the curriculum for this class and continued to expand it each year. Girls participated in fun fitness activities and learned fitness, nutrition and healthy living information.

This class was the catalyst that started the PE Fit Company & the PE Fit Nutrition & Activity Programs that now encompass upper elementary through high school as well as a college freshman and an adult wellness program.

The PE Fit Girls Program has now been presented by Betty at the National AAHPERD convention twice as well as at several state Health & Physical Education conventions. It will be an honor for Betty to present this program as the keynote speaker at the Alaska State AAHPERD convention in October 2009.

Betty continues to keep fit and healthy by training for marathons & half marathons as well as through swimming, biking, yoga, strength training, hiking and other fun fitness activities! Betty strives to be an example of healthy living to her family, friends, students and church.

Nutrition & Activity Program for Teen Girls
Table of Contents

Course Intro for Girls...	7
Personal Info & Goal Sheets...	9
Article summary forms...	13
First Quarter	**15**
Distance Challenge	16
Nutrition Basics/Food Guide Pyramid	17
Food Pyramid Questions	21
Serving Size/Portion Control	25
Meals/Snacks/Restaurant Assignment	27
Fitness Basics + Questions	33
Weight Gain & Weight Loss	41
Disease Prevention + Questions	44
Personal Health	53
Journal Pages First Quarter	58
Second Quarter	**83**
Ab/Push-up Challenge	84
Lifestyle Evaluations	85
Looking Back & Goal Setting	90
Self-Image/Body-Image	93
Body Type & Fashion	97
Eating Disorders	103
Family, Friends & Relationships	106
Exercise & Pregnancy	109
Healthy Living	113
Lifestyle Evaluations & Questions	115
Journal Pages Second Quarter	121
Workouts	145

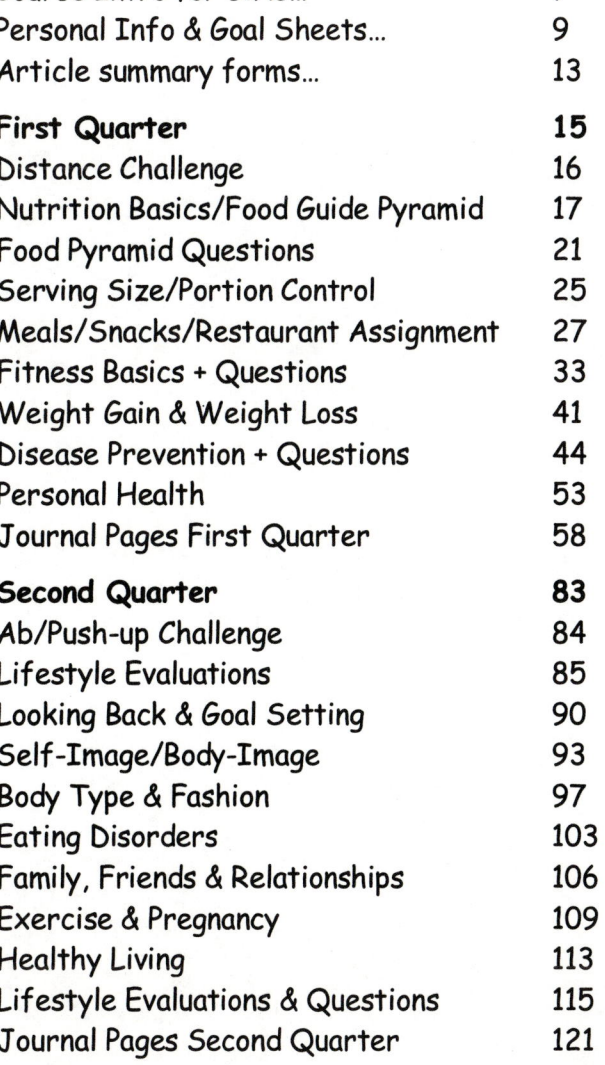

Nutrition & Activity Program
for
Teen Girls

Program Goals:

- ❖ Provide nutrition, fitness and health information to teen girls enabling them to make informed lifestyle decisions
- ❖ Provide a "safe" environment for self expression through class discussion of topics and issues important to young women
- ❖ Provide an accepting, non-competitive atmosphere where girls feel confident or gain confidence in their physical abilities to participate in fitness activities in class and at home
- ❖ Provide an opportunity to achieve fitness goals that may seem unattainable
- ❖ Encourage young women to learn and try new fitness activities which will in turn help them grow in self-confidence and self-esteem in all areas
- ❖ Encourage healthy eating habits through practical advice
- ❖ Encourage participation in "Challenges" for fun and to improve fitness levels
- ❖ Examine current habits through the journal activities and track positive changes
- ❖ Focus on self-improvement and celebration of individual differences
- ❖ Connect with students on an individual basis
- ❖ Create an environment that allows the "girls" to be comfortable with each other, the teacher and themselves
- ❖ Demonstrate that FITNESS CAN BE FUN!

Nutrition & Activity Class
for Teen Girls

Welcome to an exciting new adventure at your high school! This class is a unique opportunity for high school girls to **work together** to meet personal fitness goals, learn more about themselves, fitness, nutrition, weight training, yoga and other fitness activities.

The focus of this class is on **fitness** not weight loss. If it is your goal to lose weight, we will work toward that goal with an emphasis on good nutrition and exercise as a means of achieving weight loss. However, we will not be "dieting" as a part of this class. It is the opinion of many experts in the field of exercise science that an increase in activity and healthy eating habits will help an individual achieve their optimum fitness level and body weight. We will be discussing nutrition and healthy eating habits.

The goal of this class is to help each girl meet her personal fitness goals. Therefore, feedback from each young lady is essential for the success of the class on a personal level. In order to facilitate the feedback, **each student will be required to keep a personal fitness/nutrition journal.** This journal will be checked each week to ensure that it is completed on a regular basis. **The journal will count for 25% of the student's grade each grading period.**

Class participation is 50% of your grade! Each student is expected to dress for class daily and participate in the activity planned. If a student is at school and chooses not to participate in class for the day or is not prepared for class, she will be expected to read an article on a fitness related topic, write a summary of the article and turn it in to the teacher. The student will have two days to complete the article summary. **Each student may turn in a maximum of 3 journal articles without penalty to her grade.** Additional articles must be written for days that she does not participate but after three her grade will be affected.

Each student is expected to come dressed for the activity planned and bring any necessary equipment or material with her to class. This would include athletic shoes, shorts or athletic pants, T-shirts or appropriate tank tops and sweatshirt or jacket. Dress for class should be modest and should not expose cleavage or abdomen. Shorts should not be too short. Bring weather appropriate clothing to walk/run outside on a regular basis. An activity schedule will be provided so you can be prepared with appropriate equipment/clothing.

"Classroom" participation and assignments are 25% of the grade! There will be "classroom" sessions at least every other week in this class. We will discuss fitness related topics including nutrition, metabolism, osteoporosis, exercise type and intensity, issues concerning women and exercise, disease prevention through exercise and other related topics. Each student is responsible for the material covered in each lesson and for any assignments on the topic. There may also be a short quiz on a topic that is discussed.

Personal Training Information Sheet

Name _____ Shoe size _____
Grade _____   T-shirt size _____
Homeroom _____   Birthday _____
Address _____   Study Hall _____
City _____ Zip _____
Phone number _____ Cell _____
Parent's names _____

Goals for this class: _____
_____
_____

Fitness Goals: _____
_____

Nutrition/Weight Goals: _____
_____

Extra-Curricular Activities: _____
_____

Tell me something about yourself: _____
_____

Do you have any physical limitations for exercise? _____
_____

Turn in to teacher!

Personal Goals

This class is designed to help you meet your personal goals for fitness, nutrition and weight loss, if desired.
Below, please list your goals for this semester regarding fitness, nutrition, academics, extracurricular activities & weight loss.

Fitness Goals: _____

_____

_____

Nutrition Goals: _____

_____

_____

Academic Goals: _____

_____

_____

Extracurricular Activities: _____

_____

_____

Weight Loss Goals: _____

_____

Turn in to teacher!

Personal Goals

This class is designed to help you meet your personal goals for fitness, nutrition and weight loss, if desired.
Below, please list your goals for this semester regarding fitness, nutrition, academics, extracurricular activities & weight loss.

Fitness Goals: _____
_____
_____

Nutrition Goals: _____
_____
_____

Academic Goals: _____
_____
_____

Extracurricular Activities: _____
_____
_____

Weight Loss Goals: _____
_____

Keep in journal for your reference!

Article Summary Form

Name _____   Date_____

Date of class missed _____

Title of article _____

Magazine or Journal _____

Issue Number _____ Date _____ Pages _____

Author of article _____

Please answer the following questions for the article that you read on fitness or nutrition today. Please answer the questions in complete sentences using proper grammar and punctuation.

1. What interested you about this article?
2. What is the main theme of the article?
3. What did you learn from this article? List at least three things.
4. How can you apply what you learned to your life? Please give examples.
5. Is the information from a reliable source? Is it reasonable?

_____
_____
_____
_____
_____
_____
_____
_____
_____
_____

14

1st Quarter
Getting started!

DISTANCE CHALLENGE

What?
Walk or run _____ miles

When??
_____ through _____

Where???
In class or at home...record miles covered each day in your journal and
put up a sticker on the "Challenge Chart" for each mile!

Why?
To become more fit and challenge yourself!

PRIZES!!
Most miles completed – BIG REWARD!
Meeting the goal – reward for everyone who meets the goal!
Doubling the goal – additional reward for doubling the goal!

Let's get started!

MyPyramid.gov

In this journal, you are going to keep track of the food that you eat and the food group to which it belongs. There is a place for you to check off the number of servings that you eat from each food group. You are aiming for 3 servings from each of the food groups. That is one represented at each meal. Or a total of 18 portions of different foods daily spread over breakfast, lunch, dinner and two snacks.   As you will see in your first assignment, you may require more servings from a particular food group. However, as you get started, you will aim for at least 3 servings from each of the different food groups and then add to it if necessary.

Why keep track of your nutritional habits?
- *build better habits
- *recognize food choices
- *identify food groups where you might be deficient
- *track positive changes that you are making

The Food Guide Pyramid:
The Federal Government has developed a new Food Guide Pyramid. It is designed to meet individual needs better. There is a terrific web site that has been created for you to assess your needs based on the new pyramid. You will enter you age, gender and activity level and it will tell you your daily requirements for each of the food groups.

Your first assignment:
1. Go to the web site MyPyramid.gov and go to the section 'My Pyramid' and enter your information to determine your daily needs.   Print out the information on your pyramid needs, put your name on it and turn it in!
2. Complete the questions about the food groups in the food group pyramid section in your journal. (pages 21-24)

You may find that you need more from the grain group or from the fruit group than the 3 servings that we are aiming for initially.
So you should aim to eat the number of servings that you require.

This assignment is due _____!
Let your instructor know if you have any questions or problems accessing the site!

What is it??

Carbohydrates (CHO):

Carbohydrates are fuel for the body! We need them!! Eating more whole grain carbohydrates will cause fewer sugar cravings since CHOs are a natural source of sugar. If the body does not get enough whole grain CHOs, then it will crave sugary snacks like candies, cookies, cakes, etc. Look for foods that contain at least 3 grams of fiber per serving. Essential nutrients found in whole grain CHOs include fiber and B vitamins. Most whole grain carbohydrates are low in fat and calories...just be careful with what you put on them (cream cheese, cheese, sour cream, etc.). Try to start incorporating some healthy whole grain CHOs into your diet. You might be surprised how good they are!

Examples of carbohydrates: breads, cereals, pasta, potatoes, rice crackers, fruit and starchy vegetables (carrots, turnips, parsnips, beets, peas, squash, corn), popcorn, oatmeal, and crackers, etc.

Protein (Meat and bean group):

Proteins are an essential nutrient for life. They are the primary component of the brain, heart, blood, skin and hair. You also need protein to build and repair muscle. Protein foods also give a satisfying effect to a meal because they take longer to break down and go into the blood stream.

Examples of protein foods: beef, liver, pork, chicken, turkey, fish, eggs, cheese, peanut butter, sausage, deli meats, hot dogs, lamb, dried beans, peas, lentils and nuts.

Aim for 2/3 to 3/4 of a meal to be CHO and 1/3 to 1/4 of the meal protein.

Dairy:

Milk and other dairy products are rich sources of calcium, an essential bone building material. Bone mass builds through the teen years. So it is especially important for people through their teens and early twenties to get enough calcium on a daily basis. Aim for at least 4 to 6 servings of dairy products a day! (By the way, each can of pop that you drink robs your body of 100 mg of calcium)

Examples of dairy products: milk, ice cream, yogurt, cheese, etc.

Fats/Oils:

Fats are essential for a healthy body! They help you absorb fat-soluble vitamins A, D, E, and K. Fats also are needed to support the energy needed for normal growth and development of healthy cells. It is important to eat healthy fats and avoid the "bad fats". The ones to look out for include any "partially hydrogenated oils" or trans fats as well as other saturated fats...stay away from these!

Healthy/Good Fats: olives and olive oil, peanut butter, nuts, canola oil, avocado, flaxseed and flaxseed oil.

Bad Fats: trans fat, butter, margarine, partially hydrogenated oils, and fried foods.

Fruits and Veggies:

Eat any fruits or vegetables that you love and consider trying a few new ones. Raw, fresh, frozen, canned, dehydrated, 100% juice, etc. all count! You can eat almost as many fruits or veggies as you want. They contain lots of vitamins and minerals for a minimum of calories and fat!

Discretionary Calories:

Discretionary calories are the "extra calories" that include higher caloric choices from a food group. Foods that contribute to discretionary calories are whole milk, cheese, sweets, candy, soft drinks, desserts, donuts, fast food, fried food, junk food, etc.

Weight Control a USA Problem

One of the problems with weight control in the USA is the use of super-sized portions in our restaurants and fast food places. According to the USDA, Americans are eating 150 more calories per day than they were 20 years ago and that adds up to an extra 15 pounds per year. This increased portion size then carries over into our everyday eating habits even when not at a restaurant. The chart below provides an example of what a serving size should look like for specific foods and food categories. When the food guide pyramid lists a serving of a given food, these guidelines are what you should follow. Most of these servings are much smaller than you are used to eating! One method for estimating serving size is to compare it to different parts of your hand. Obviously everyone's hands are not the same size but usually the hand size "fits" the person's body size.

Food	What a serving should look like!
Meat, Fish, or Poultry	Palm of your hand (3 ounces)
Mixed Nuts	1 Layer on the palm of your hand (1/4 cup)
Veggies or Berries	A tight fist (1 cup)
Popcorn or Cereal	2 Cupped hands or 2 handfuls (1 cup)
Cooked Pasta	1 Rounded handful (1/2 cup)
Cheese	2 Lengths of index finger (2 ounces)
Butter, Salad Dressing or Oil	Finger tip (1/2 tsp)
Peanut Butter	3 Thumb tips (2 Tbsp)
Fruits	Tennis ball or the size that fits in your closed hand
Non-Starchy Vegetables	Baseball or two cupped hands
Natural Carbohydrates (rice, pasta, cereal, etc.)	Your cupped hand
Bread or Sandwich; cheese	Computer disc
Peanut Butter, Healthy Fats (olive oil, salad dressing)	An Oreo cookie
Bagel - small	Six ounce can of tuna
Lean Dairy Foods - milk, ice cream or yogurt	Your fist
Muffins - small	Tennis ball
Mashed Potatoes	Your cupped hand
Fruit Juice	Container of yogurt
Potato Chips or Pretzels	Your cupped hand
Pancake or Waffle	Palm of your hand
Cheese	4 dice

Food Pyramid Questions

Name _____

Grain Group

1. What is the difference between whole grains and refined grains?

2. What does it mean if a refined grain has been enriched?

3. List three health benefits of eating grains.

4. List three nutrients derived from eating grain foods.

5. Give five examples of what would count as a one ounce equivalent from the grain group.

6. Give two examples of what you should look for on a label to determine if it is a "whole grain" product.

7. Give two tips to help you increase the amount of whole grains that you eat.

Vegetable Group

1. List the five subgroups of vegetables and give two examples in each subgroup.

2. List three health benefits from eating a diet rich in vegetables.

2. List three nutrients found in vegetables and what their function is in the body.

4. Give five examples (one from each subgroup) that would count as one-cup serving.

5. Give three tips to help you eat more vegetables.

Fruit Group

1. What are your three favorite fruits?

2. List three health benefits of eating a diet rich in fruit.

3. List three nutrients found in fruit and tell what each nutrient does for you.

4. Give three examples of a one cup serving of fruit.

5. List four tips to help you eat more fruit.

Oils

1. What are oils?

2. Do oils from plant sources contain cholesterol?

3. What kind of fats tend to raise "bad" (LDL) cholesterol levels in the blood?

Name _____

4. List four types of oils that you regularly consume.

Milk Group

1. How many glasses of milk do you have daily on a regular basis?

2. Give three examples of a serving from the milk group.

3. List two health benefits that are derived from consuming dairy products.

4. List three nutrients that are found in dairy products and describe the role they play in keeping us healthy.

5. Why is it important to make fat-free or low-fat choices from the milk group?

6. List three tips for making wise choices from the dairy group.

7. Give three suggestions for including calcium in the diet of a person who cannot consume milk products.

Meat and Beans Groups

1. Why is it important to include fish, nuts and seeds in your diet?

2. List five selections from the meat and beans group.

3. What foods are the richest sources of vitamin E in this food group?

4. Give three examples of a one-ounce serving from the meat and beans group.

5. List three nutrients derived from the meat and bean group and their function in the body.

6. What foods in this group should be limited in order to keep the "bad" cholesterol called LDL (low-density lipoprotein) cholesterol level in a healthy range?

7. List three tips to help you make wise choices from the meat and bean group.

8. What are some choices in the meat and bean group for vegetarians?

Discretionary Calories

1. What are discretionary calories?

2. How can you use your discretionary calorie allowance?

3. List six foods that would contribute to discretionary calories due to their high fat or sugar content.

Physical Activity

1. List three moderate physical activities.

2. List three vigorous physical activities.

3. What is the minimum number of minutes a day that you should exercise?

4. List four reasons that physical activity is important.

6. List two types of physical activity and their health benefits.

7. About how many minutes of exercise per day may be needed to prevent weight gain?

8. List five tips for increasing your daily physical activity.

Application

1. After determining your needs from the food guide pyramid and answering the questions in this section, use this information to analyze your current dietary habits. Are you meeting the requirements? Where are your weak spots? What areas need improvement?

2. Can you think of a bad nutrition habit that you currently have? Decide to drop one or two of those habits! Start with small steps that you can live with. Don't try to change everything at once! List one or two habits you will work on changing!

3. Are you meeting the requirements for physical activity for good health?

4. If you are not meeting the minimum requirements, how can you add in more daily physical activity? Start small with something you can and will do!

What did you find out at MyPyramid.gov? Name _____

What are your nutrition recommendations from the Food Guide Pyramid?

Grains	Fruits	Vegetables	Milk	Meat & Beans
_____ oz	_____ cups	_____ cups	_____ cups	_____ oz
_____ servings	_____ servings	_____ servings	_____ servings	_____ servings
1 slice of bread, 1 cup of ready-to-eat cereal, or ½ cup of cooked rice, cooked pasta, or cooked cereal can be considered as 1 ounce equivalent from the grains group.	1 cup of fruit or 100% fruit juice, or ½ cup of dried fruit can be considered as 1 cup from the fruit group	1 cup of raw or cooked vegetables or vegetable juice, or 2 cups of raw leafy greens can be considered as 1 cup from the vegetable group	1 cup of milk or yogurt, 1 ½ ounces of natural cheese, or 2 ounces of processed cheese can be considered as 1 cup from the milk group.	1 ounce of meat, poultry or fish, ¼ cup cooked dry beans, 1 egg, 1 tablespoon of peanut butter, or ½ ounce of nuts or seeds can be considered as 1 ounce serving from the meat and beans group
Aim for at least ½ of your grains to be whole grain	Try some new fruits and don't eat the same ones all the time!	Vary your veggies… dark green, orange, starchy, dry beans & peas, etc.!	Remember low-fat choices are best!	Protein is so important… don't skimp on it!

Serving Size ➔ Weight Control

Eating the correct amount of servings and serving size of foods will help you maintain your weight and grow properly!

If weight control is a problem for you,

Check your serving sizes…are they close to what they should be?

Are you eating too many servings?

Remember that you don't want to skip any meals because it affects your <u>metabolism</u>!

To keep your body functioning at its best, eat three meals a day and a healthy low-fat snack or two!

What happens when you slow your metabolism down by skipping meals?   What can you do to boost your metabolism?

Making Comparisons... and Better Choices

*It is always better to eat fresh unprocessed foods
but if you are going to eat processed foods,
think about serving sizes and compare calories!
Small changes really make a big difference!*

Need something sweet?

Fruit is always best...but for candy think about these:

1 Tootsie Pop	60 Calories
1 bag of M & M's	230 calories
Movie size M & M's	770 calories
1 Hershey Bar	240 calories
9 Hershey Kisses	220 calories
1 Snickers	280 calories
Snack size candy	30-80 calories each

Snacks to Compare:

Microwave Popcorn 1 cup	35 calories
Light Popcorn 1 cup	20 calories
Buttered Popcorn 1 cup	70 calories
Healthy Choice Buttered Popcorn	16 calories
Movie Theater	60 calories/cup
Potato Chips (15 chips)	150 calories
Corn Chips (15 chips)	152 calories
Nacho Chips (15 chips)	150 calories

Ice Cream: (1/2 cup)

Vanilla	132 calories
Chocolate	143 calories
Butter pecan	310 calories
Chocolate Chip	270 calories
Vanilla Fudge	290 calories
Cookies & Cream	270 calories

"Eat This, Not That," books are great resources for food comparisons!

Fast Foods to Compare:

Soft Drink	Coke	8 oz. 100 calories	20 oz. 250 calories
French Fries	Wendy's	Small 280 calories	Biggie 490 calories
	McDonald's	Small 210 calories	Large 540 calories
Frosty	Wendy's	Small 330 calories	Large 540 calories
Milkshake	McDonald's	Small 430 calories	Large 1,130 calories
Milkshake	Burger King	Small 410 calories	Large 830 calories
Hamburger	McDonald's	Regular 260 calories	Quarter Pounder 420 calories
	Burger King	Regular 320 calories	Dbl Whopper 920 calories
Chicken Nuggets	McDonald's	6 piece 250 calories	10 piece 420 calories
Chicken Selects	McDonald's	3 pieces 380 calories	5 pieces 630 calories

Combo Meals ➔ Dining Disaster

McD's Big Mac, M Fries, M Coke	1120 calories	46gm fat	1200mg sodium
Wendy's Classic single, Biggie Fries, M Coke	1040 calories	44gm fat	1370mg sodium
BK's Whopper, M Fries, M Coke	1260 calories	60gm fat	1660mg sodium

FOOD!

*"Food is one of the most important things you'll ever buy. And yet most people never bother to think about their food and where it comes from. People spend a lot more time worrying about what kind of blue jeans to wear, what kind of video games to play, what kind of computers to buy. They compare the different models and styles, they talk to friends about various options, they read as much as they can before making a choice. But those purchases don't really matter. When you get tired of old blue jeans, video games, and computers, you just give them away or throw them out. **The food you eat enters your body and literally becomes part of you. It helps determine whether you'll be short or tall, weak or strong, thin or fat. It helps determine whether you will enjoy a long healthy life or die young.** Food is of fundamental importance. So why is it that most people don't think about fast food (or processed food) and don't know much about it!"*   Eric Schlosser & Charles Wilson, <u>Chew on This</u>, 2006

FOOD…You need to think about it!

Eating three meals a day plus snacks is your goal!
Think about the food choices you make!
Good fuel for your body helps you to think more clearly and concentrate, improve your grades, have more energy, look healthier, perform better in sports, have enough energy to exercise, stay healthy, have a positive attitude, and enjoy life more!

Breakfast…why eat it?

1. Breakfast wakes up your metabolism, which fuels your brain and muscles and helps your body burn more calories all day long!
2. Breakfast will give you the energy you need to perform well in school and athletics.

Breakfast ideas:
- → You don't have to eat breakfast foods; just choose something healthy to start your day!
- → Throw out the sugary cereals! Try whole grain cereals such as oatmeal, Cheerios, Great Grains, Wheat Chex, or Grape Nut Flakes.
- → Top a whole grain pancake or waffle with peanut butter and banana slices or other fruit or warm applesauce. Use only real maple syrup but use sparingly because it still packs a lot of calories.
- → Top quick oatmeal with nuts and fruit!
- → Make a breakfast burrito! Use a whole wheat or corn tortilla, egg, low-fat shredded cheese, veggies, beans, and salsa!
- → Melt low-fat cheese over a whole grain bagel or english muffin and team it up with 100% fruit juice!
- → Make a smoothie with fresh or frozen fruit, low-fat yogurt or milk, and ice! Eat some nuts with this to add protein!
- → Top whole-wheat toast with peanut butter! Add a glass of milk and an apple to round out the meal!
- → Even a sandwich works for breakfast…try peanut butter and jelly or banana, a real turkey or roast beef sandwich with cheese, or a toasted cheese sandwich.
- → Left-overs from dinner work well in the morning also (left-over pizza is a great breakfast!).

Do you have any ideas for healthy breakfasts that are not listed above?   *What do you usually eat for breakfast?*

Lunch...make it healthy!

Eating a healthy lunch is especially important at school!
You need energy to think clearly and concentrate in class as well as to go to practice or work!
Try to include something from each of the food groups in your lunch!

Lunch ideas:
- → Include a lean protein, vegetable, whole grain, fruit for dessert, beverage, and condiments.
- → Drink water, nonfat milk, or 100% fruit juice.
- → Eat fruit for dessert most days of the week.
- → Try to have veggies or a salad with lunch, even when you have pizza.
- → Try a whole grain pita bread stuffed with veggies and salad dressing (pack this separately).
- → Eat a peanut butter sandwich with banana or with strawberries, granola, or apples.
- → Try a wrap sandwich. Spread a tortilla with hummus, add sliced veggies: cucumber, squash,
        zucchini, peppers, lettuce, and tomatoes. Top this with cheese or avocado then roll tightly or slice.
- → Instead of processed lunch meats, try sliced turkey or roast beef slices from the deli.
- → Pack a hard-boiled egg, whole grain crackers, carrot sticks, and grapes.
- → Pack snacks for after school if you are staying for practice, to study or going to work.
- → If you want something sweet, make homemade cookies or brownies from real ingredients, not a box mix!
- → Include a yogurt for calcium, just be sure to keep it cold.
- → Take along water or juice!

If you eat in the cafeteria, make conscientious decisions about what you eat! There are healthier alternatives...don't make excuses for poor food choices.   Whatever you do...DO NOT EAT FROM THE VENDING MACHINES FOR LUNCH OR SNACKS! You can save money and tons of calories by planning ahead for your lunch and snacks! LIMIT THE AMOUNT OF FAST FOOD YOU EAT FOR LUNCH OR SNACKS! If you decide to go for fast food, go with a plan in mind and know what you are getting! Take the time to look up your favorite fast food restaurant on the web and get the nutrition information.

Dinner (supper)...family time!

Research has shown that when families eat together, they make better food choices and build relationships.
Try to eat with your family several times a week if possible.

- → Plan a menu and shopping list with your family or friends
- → Try to eat something from all food groups
- → Use smaller plates for portion control...no seconds
- → Use fruit, nonfat yogurt, or nuts as a dessert
- → Drink water or milk
- → Eat homemade desserts rather than store bought
- → Eat less packaged foods; this will help reduce the amount of fat,
        calories, sodium, and chemicals in your diet
- → Keep it simple...good dinners do not have to be complicated; just use fresh, real foods

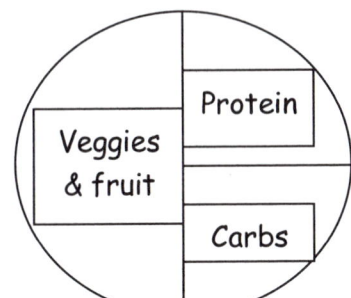

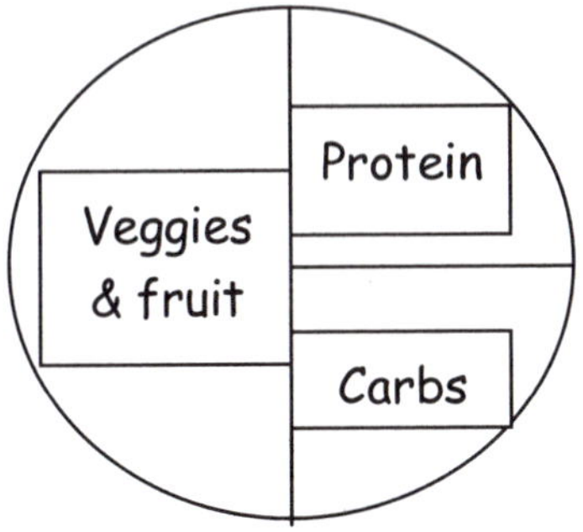

Snacks…you probably need one!

Try to combine a healthy carbohydrate (fruit, whole wheat bagel, whole wheat crackers, granola, raisins, etc.) with a high quality protein (nuts, yogurt, milk, peanut butter, hummus, egg, etc.).
The carbohydrates give energy for now and the protein helps you stay full longer!

Snack ideas:
- Whole-grain crackers and tuna or cheese
- Peanut butter or cashew butter with celery or apples
- Rice cakes topped with apple butter, peanut butter & jelly, or cream cheese
- Real chicken or turkey wrapped in a whole grain tortilla
- Lettuce and veggies with hummus wrapped in a tortilla
- Whole grain cereal with low-fat milk
- Applesauce (try making homemade…it's great)
- Low-fat yogurt with granola or sunflower seeds
- Cheese cubes and a handful of grapes
- Frozen grapes…especially if it is hot outside
- 100% fruit popsicles

- Bananas with peanut butter
- Raisins and nuts
- Corn tortilla sprinkled with low-fat cheese (broil to melt)
- Pineapple chunks with lean turkey slices
- Apples with yogurt
- Hummus with sliced veggies
- Homemade fruit smoothie
- Fresh fruit or veggies with a low-fat dip
- Fruit salad
- Popcorn, lightly salted and lightly buttered

Why is it so important to eat three meals plus a snack? Why shouldn't you skip breakfast and lunch?

One reason you shouldn't go long periods of time without eating is that is will affect your metabolism.
Metabolism is the number of calories your body burns at rest.
When you don't eat for a long period of time (example: from dinner to lunch the next day…16-18+ hours) and this is a regular habit, your body goes into "starvation mode" and slows down your metabolism to conserve energy.
Our bodies were designed to do this in case of situations where we had to go without food or eat only a little food for an extended period of time.
Can you think of a time in history where this slowing of your metabolism would have been helpful or necessary for survival?

You do not want to do anything to slow down your metabolism! Eating regular meals and snacks will help keep your body running well and supply all the vitamins, minerals, and nutrients that you need! You will also have a lot more energy when you eat at regular intervals!

If you are having trouble with weight management, try eating three healthy, well-balanced meals a day and a fruit or veggie snack and you will keep your metabolism up and burn more calories all day long! Add in some exercise each day and your weight problems may disappear!

Remember to watch your portion size…refer to the chart in the food pyramid section (page 19) for a reference of serving sizes!

Restaurant Assignment

Name_____

Have you ever wondered if your favorite restaurant meal is healthy? Maybe you don't want to know!

Your assignment:
> Visit the web site of your favorite restaurant and record the information for your favorite meal.
> Include everything that you would eat and drink with this meal.
> The web site should list all ingredients, condiments, and options with calorie count, grams of fat, sodium and other nutrients.
> Print out any information that you can on the meal of your choice and staple it to this assignment.
> In the table below, record your favorite restaurant and meal with nutrition information.

Restaurant	
Web site	
Favorite Meal	
Total Calories	
Total Grams of Fat	
Total Milligrams of Sodium	
Based on what you have learned in this class, is this meal healthy?	
What changes could you make to this meal to improve its nutritional value?	

32

Fitness Basics

Benefits of Exercise:

- Relieves stress...improves your mood
- Improves endurance, reduces fatigue
- Lowers blood pressure
- Helps ease symptoms of PMS
- Prevents certain kinds of cancer
- Improves self-image, self-esteem and body-image
- Provides for greater mental focusing skills
- Heightens sensitivity to our body's needs
- Gives us a greater peace of mind and ability to relax.
- Slows down the aging process...unused muscles shrink about 10% each decade.
- Upper body strength lets us "carry our own weight" in the world...lift children, carry heavy items, move furniture etc.
- Eases misalignments and muscle imbalances in our bodies.
- Improves problem areas in posture...we stand taller and look leaner.
- Changes your body shape...by toning muscles.
- Decreases the risk of contracting health problems associated with high levels of body fat, such as heart disease (#1 killer of men and women in the USA), diabetes and cancer.
- Helps us stay lean. Muscle is active tissue that burns up more calories than fat. As energy needs increase, metabolism speeds up and we have to eat more, more often. Not to worry though, as long as our meals are low fat and small, weight loss and improved levels of fitness will happen.
- Builds muscle...muscle weighs more than fat...so don't depend on the scale as a measure of success or failure. The way your clothes fit and how tight your muscles feel is a better indication of fitness results.

Essential Elements of Fitness

The secret to improving your current level of fitness or maintaining a high level of fitness is variety in your workouts. Your body is amazing and will adapt to a given level of exercise or activity over time. So after a while the same workout will not continue to produce results for you! In order to get the fitness results you desire, you will not only need to include the three main fitness components as you design your workouts...aerobic, strength and flexibility exercises...but you must also manipulate the frequency, intensity and time of the exercises.

Fitness Components*

Aerobic/Cardiovascular Exercise
Strength Training for Muscular Power & Endurance
Flexibility Exercises
Body Composition

*these are explained on the following pages!

Exercise Routine Sequence

Warm-up: start with light exercise...jogging, fast walking, jump rope, etc. to warm up muscles slowly for 3-5 minutes. Stretch muscles lightly to loosen up and prepare for the exercise of the day.

Exercise of the day: aerobic or strength training or both. Begin at a lower intensity and build up to the desired intensity level.

Cool-down: it is important to give the body a chance to cool down or recover from exercise to allow the blood flow, heart rate and breathing to return to normal. Slow down the activity or walk to recover. Stretch muscles more thoroughly than prior to exercise. Drink fluids and consume a small snack within a reasonable amount of time to refuel the body.

F.I.T.T.E.E. Principle - to improve your level of physical fitness you must continually change up the exercise or activity you perform. These changes can be facilitated through manipulating the components of Frequency, Intensity, Time, and Type of the activity or exercise.

Frequency –how **often** you exercise

Intensity – how **hard** you are working

Time – the **length** of your exercise session

Type – the **type** of exercise you do...running, biking, yoga, weights, etc.

Enjoyment – **do** you enjoy this type of exercise?

Effectiveness – is the exercise plan working for you...are you seeing results?

Questions to consider when determining the frequency, intensity, time, type and enjoyment of the activity or exercise of choice:
- → What is your current level of fitness?
- → What are your goals for the activity or health?
- → How hard are you working (intensity)?

- → How often are you working out...daily, weekly, etc. (frequency)?
- → What is the length of your exercise session (time)?
- → Is this an activity you enjoy and will participate in consistently?

Aerobic/Cardiovascular Exercise

When you exercise aerobically, large amounts of blood and oxygen are supplied to the muscles, tissues and organs to meet the increased demands of exercise. **The supply of oxygen meets the body's demand for oxygen**...of course that means you will be breathing hard and sweating!

Examples of Cardiovascular or Aerobic Exercise: walking, hiking, running/jogging, swimming, cycling, cross-country skiing, dancing, skipping rope, rowing, stair climbing, in-line skating, endurance games, etc.

Benefits of Aerobic Exercise:
- strengthens the heart muscle making it more efficient
- decreases resting heart rate
- strengthens the lungs and muscles that assist in breathing
- improves the ability of the body to transport oxygen to muscles at work and at rest
- reduces or prevents high blood pressure

- improves circulation by clearing out cholesterol buildup
- teaches the body to burn fat as a primary fuel source
- improves psychological disposition...mood
- reduces stress levels
- boosts metabolism...calories burned at rest!
- tones muscles
- increases flexibility, reducing capability for injury

The frequency, duration and intensity of the aerobic exercise will influence your aerobic fitness.

In general aerobic sessions should be performed **3 to 5 days per week (frequency),** last from **20 to 60 minutes (duration)** at **varying intensity** levels.

Frequency: beginners should aim to exercise aerobically 3 to 4 days per week with the goal to work up to 6 days per week.

Time: beginners should exercise aerobically for 20 to 30 minutes per workout with the goal of working up to at least one day a week at 60+ minutes. A couple days a week, plan on exercising for a shorter amount of time and at least one day a week try extending the time at a slower pace.

Intensity: can be determined by monitoring your heart rate, breathing (talk test) or your perceived exertion. In order to gain benefits from aerobic exercise, you must exercise at an intensity level that raises your heart rate and breathing rate...in other words you need to be breathing hard and sweating! One way to determine the intensity of your effort is to **monitor your heart rate.** If you are fortunate enough to have a heart rate monitor, this is a convenient device to use. There are some new formulas for determining maximum heart rate but we will use the simplest one at this point.

Maximum Heart Rate: Maximum HR = 220 – age   Your Maximum HR = 220 - _____ = _____

*the easiest way to measure heart rate is to count for 6 seconds and multiply by 10!

Intensity Level	Low	Medium	High
Target Heart Rate	55%-70%	70%-80%	80%-90%
Your Target Heart Rates			

Talk Test: you can approximate your intensity level by using the talk test during aerobic exercise. This is based on the ease of which you could talk to a friend while exercising aerobically.

Low Intensity: can easily carry on a conversation with a friend during the activity
Medium Intensity: more difficult to talk during the activity
High Intensity: almost impossible to talk during the activity

Perceived Exertion: a scale from 1-10 that provides a reference for the intensity of your exercise effort.
Example of scale...adapted for you!
1 – watching your favourite TV show & snacking
2 – easy effort...could walk at this pace all day
3 – easy effort...breathing a little harder
4 – starting to sweat...feel good & can talk easily (low intensity)
5 – easy to talk but sweating a little more and a little more difficult (low intensity)
6 – can still talk but slightly out of breath (moving towards medium intensity)
7 – could talk but don't want to waste the energy...sweating like crazy (medium intensity)
8 – would only grunt in response to a question...can only keep this pace for a short amount of time (high intensity)
9 – can't talk at all...feel like I am going to die!
10 – DONE!

GOAL FOR MOST WORKOUTS! { 5, 6 }
INTERVAL BLASTS! { 8, 9 }

Mix things up!
For example:
Two days exercise at a lower intensity for a longer time...like 30 – 45 minutes...you could talk easily while running with your friend. One day exercise at a medium intensity level for a shorter time... 20-25 minutes...a little less conversation or take turns talking. One day exercise at a higher intensity level...intervals...alternate short bouts of high intensity exercise (30 – 60 seconds) with an active recovery between (jog 60 seconds)...no talking only lots of sweating and heavy breathing!

Anaerobic Exercise

Although not listed among the fitness components, anaerobic exercise can be used in conjunction with aerobic exercise to help boost calorie burning and intensity of an exercise session. Short bursts of high intensity exercise intermixed with lower intensity exercise is called **interval training**. Athletes employ interval training; however, it is a useful tool for anyone to improve fitness. Interval training example: after a warm-up, run for 2 minutes at a comfortable pace, sprint for 30 - 60 seconds, jog for 2 minutes, repeating several times finishing with a jog for at least 5 minutes.

Anaerobic Exercise– the body's demand for oxygen exceeds its ability to supply oxygen and therefore incurs an oxygen debt.
- this oxygen debt requires the body to work hard to provide enough oxygen...so you burn more calories
- usually associated with improvements in muscular strength, endurance, power and flexibility
- lasts less than 2 minutes or is intermittent with bouts of aerobic exercise (intervals)

Examples of Anaerobic Exercises: sprinting, swimming sprints, short fasts burst on an elliptical or bike, lifting a heavy object, explosive exercises.

Strength Training

Definition: Trains and develops the muscles for power and endurance.

Power is the ability of the muscles to do a maximum work within the shortest amount of time.

Endurance is the ability of the muscles to do moderate work over an extended period of time.

Benefits:
- → Increases muscle strength
- → Increases bone density
- → Reduces body fat
- → Improves posture
- → Helps control blood pressure
- → Raises Basal Metabolic Rate and increases daily calorie expenditure
- → Injury prevention from normal activities
- → Improves physical appearance
- → Increases tendon and ligament thickness - helps with joint stability
- → Reduces anxiety and depression and improves self-efficacy and overall psychological well being…confidence & mood
- → Improves glucose tolerance - which may help to prevent diabetes, coronary artery disease, cataracts, stroke, retinopathy and reduces risk of infection.

Sets and Repetitions:

Repetition is referred to as a **"rep"** and is a single lift of weights.

Set is a group of reps. An exercise is generally composed of 3 to 4 sets.

Goals: **Building Muscle:** 6 to 8 reps should be done with a heavier weight

Toning or Maintaining Fitness Level: 12 to 16 reps should be done with a lighter weight.

Weekly Requirements:

The ACSM (American College of Sports Medicine) recommends at least one set of <u>8-12 repetitions</u> of <u>8-10 exercises</u> that work the major muscle groups at least <u>twice a week</u>.

Reps	Weights	Results	Rest Period between Sets
6-8	Heavy	Builds muscle at the fastest rate	2-3 minutes
8-12	Medium	Building/Toning Muscle	1 minute
12-16	Light	Toning Muscle	30 seconds or less

Flexibility Exercises

Benefits:
- ✓ reduces the chance of injury
- ✓ maintains range of motion of the joints
- ✓ promotes good posture
- ✓ reduces tension

Instructions/Precautions:
- ✓ Cold muscles should never be stretched…warm-up the muscles before stretching…
- ✓ Stretching before exercise…after a warm-up… reduces the potential for injury by warming up and lengthening muscles & connective tissue.
- ✓ Stretching after exercise reverses the tightening and shortening effect of exercise on the muscles used.
- ✓ NEVER BOUNCE DURING A STRETCH OR PERFORM A FORCED STRETCH!!! In the past, coaches/trainers/teachers advised people to bounce during a stretch to help them increase flexibility. This practice does not work because of a protective built in reflex within our muscles. The <u>stretch reflex</u> is the body's involuntary response to forcing or bouncing to stretch muscles further. It causes the muscle to immediately shorten in a spring-like manner to protect from over stretching. Gentle, slow and controlled stretching will achieve results.

Fueling for Exercise

In order to have enough energy to complete your workout as well as achieve the desired results and fully recover from your effort, you have to fuel your body properly! Many books have been written on fueling your body for exercise. If you are out to achieve your maximum potential for sport participation, you may want to invest the time to study the recommendations by nutritionists and doctors. Nancy Clark's <u>Sport's Nutrition Bible</u> is an excellent resource.

For the rest of us a few simple guidelines should suffice:

- Consume a complex carbohydrate snack before exercise, such as: whole wheat bagel, toast, crackers, banana, apple, rice, cereal, etc.
- Timing the snack can be tricky…experiment to see what works for you!
- As a general rule the snack should be eaten 1-2 hours before exercise. Your working muscles will be using most of the blood flow during exercise so digestion will be slowed…causing that snack to lay in the stomach feeling like a brick if eaten too close to the workout!
- Drink plenty of water throughout the day and during exercise…especially in the heat! Drink at least a few gulps of water every 15-20 minutes throughout your workout to keep properly hydrated.
- Sports drinks are not necessary for exercise lasting less than one hour.
- After the workout consume a protein/carb snack within a reasonable amount of time such as: yogurt & granola, peanuts & raisins, peanut butter & banana, PBJ sandwich, chocolate milk, etc.
- Drink at least 8 ounces of water after your workout and continue to rehydrate throughout the day/evening.

Body Composition

→ A measure of fitness or health based on the amount of body fat and lean tissue
→ It is dangerous to be too thin as well as too heavy
→ Too much body fat increases the risk of developing diabetes, high blood pressure, high cholesterol, and cardiovascular disease and some cancers.

Percent Body Fat: can be found using devices such as a scale that measures body fat, a bioelectrical impedance device or skin-fold calipers.

The reliability of the body fat percentage will be dependent upon the following factors:

- Age of the device
- Experience of the person using the device
- Accuracy of input data
- Level of hydration
- Time of day

A more accurate comparison of progress will be achieved when conditions are closely duplicated.

Classification	Women % Body Fat	Men % Body Fat
Essential Fat	10-14 %	2-4%
Athletes	17-20%	6-13%
Fitness	20-24%	14-17%
Acceptable	24-25%	18-20%
Overweight	26-29.9%	21-24.9%
Obese	> 30%	> 25%

Notice that women have a higher amount of essential body fat than men. Given a man and woman with similar fitness levels, the woman will have a higher percentage of body fat...this is not fair but normal!

Body Mass Index (BMI):

BMI is a practical tool used by health-care professionals to screen individuals for overweight and obesity. BMI is a measure of weight in relation to height. It can be a useful screening tool for teens because it only requires height and weight measurements. However, since BMI is not a direct measure of body fatness, results must be interpreted with care. Athletes and dancers often have a higher than expected BMI due to their increased muscle mass... but they are not overweight. Teen's (and children's) BMIs need to be plotted on a BMI growth chart to account for different stages of development at various ages. The BMI growth chart will provide a more accurate picture of health status.

To determine if your BMI is in a healthy range, visit the Center for Disease Control website. Enter your up-to-date height and weight information into the BMI calculator for teens.

Where you carry the excess fat is very important!

Extra fat carried around the waist increases the risk for developing disease more than fat carried on the thighs and buttocks. Therefore, keeping tabs on your waist size can be an important tool to help manage your health and risk for disease! Usually guys carry more excess weight in their stomach and women in their thighs and buttocks. However, this is not always the case...body build and genetics help determine where fat is stored! The recommended maximum waist size for women is 35 inches. If you are at or near this number, it is time to take action! Remember... every step toward your healthier body counts...just get started! So by using a simple tape measure you can get a fairly accurate picture of your health status and disease risk...here's how!

Record your waist circumference....take it around your belly button....do not suck in that stomach!

Waist Circumference _____ in.

Do you need to work on reducing your waist size?
What is the best way to reduce excess fat from your middle... aerobic exercise, abdominal exercises or both?

Overall Exercise Guidelines

Frequency Guidelines:

Activity	Frequency for Beginners	Frequency for Average to High Fitness Levels
Cardiovascular Exercise	3-5 days per week	4-6 days per week
Weight Training	1-3 days per week	3-5 days per week

Intensity Guidelines:

Activity	Intensity for Beginners	Intensity for Average to High Fitness Levels
Cardiovascular Exercise	55-70% of maximum heart rate _____ to _____ bpm Low to Medium Intensity 4 to 6 on Perceived Exertion Scale Could easily talk with a friend while exercising!	70-90% of maximum heart rate _____ to _____ bpm Medium to High Intensity 6 to 8 on Perceived Exertion Scale More difficult to talk during exercise!
Weight Training	A weight you can lift 8-12 times max!	A weight you can lift 12-15 times max!

Duration Guidelines:

Activity	Time/Duration for Beginners	Time/Duration for Average to High Fitness Levels
Cardiovascular Exercise	20-30 minutes	35 minutes to 1 hour plus
Weight Training	20-30 minutes	45 minutes to 1 hour plus

Remember to incorporate the three fitness components of aerobic, strength and flexibility exercises into your workout routines. Take at least one day off each week to allow your body to rest and recover from exercise.

Change up your workouts to continue to challenge your body by manipulating the frequency, intensity, time and type of your activities! Most importantly...HAVE FUN!

Find a friend or family member to exercise with you...it will help keep you motivated and accountable!

Fitness Basics

Name_____

1. List the three types of exercise that should be included in a fitness plan.

2. Explain the FITTEE Principle.

   F _____

   I _____

   T _____

   T _____

   E _____

   E _____

3. Why is it important to know your body composition (BMI or % body fat) along with your weight?

4. If a person is overweight, is the location of the excess fat important? Why?

5. Using the information in the Fitness Basics section, develop a personalized fitness plan for someone in your family or a friend. Include aerobic exercise, strength training, and flexibility along with the recommendations for each. Be sure to consider the current fitness level of the individual. Create an 8-week plan. Organize the plan in a simple to follow and easy to read format. This should be typed and turned in along with this paper!

Weight Gain & Weight Loss

Yes, we are actually talking about both of these issues in the same section. In this class, there are girls facing the issues of weight gain or weight loss. Some of you wish that gaining weight were your struggle. However, for the extremely thin person gaining weight is as real of a problem as losing weight is for the overweight individual. This section will offer advice for both gaining weight and losing weight. Please be patient, there may be advice given for each situation that may be of value for you! Try to walk a mile in the other person's shoes and understand the struggles she faces daily.

What if you need to gain weight?

Whether you want to gain weight to improve athletic performance, enhance your health, have more confidence, or feel more comfortable in your body, it is important to incorporate good food choices and exercise. Increasing the amount of calories in your diet without regard for the quality of the food you are eating will not yield the desired results. Likewise, weight gain without exercise will result in gaining fat not muscle... this is probably not the "look" you want to achieve.

Bottom Line: to gain weight you must consume more calories than you burn. For individuals with a high metabolism this can be difficult, especially as you add in exercise! However, it is possible! Gaining muscle weight will take patience, time, hard work, dedication, and a lot of food!

It takes approximately 2500 extra calories to gain one pound of muscle. In order to gain one pound of muscle per week and provide enough fuel for exercise, an extra 350 to 700 calories must be consumed each day.

A couple of things to keep in mind: genetics will influence how "big" one can get; all food groups are essential to provide adequate calories and nutrients for weight gain and fueling workouts; and muscles must rest in order to grow... 48 hours between workouts. You can alternate muscle groups or types of exercise to give a day's rest between workouts. Carbohydrates are important to provide the energy needed to workout.

The National Dairy Council recommends the following as minimum servings from each food group in order to gain weight:
 Dairy 4+; Meat 3+; Vegetable 6+; Fruit 4+; and Grain 16+.
 Remember correct serving sizes are indicated!

Suggestions to help you gain weight:
1. <u>Never</u> skip a meal...eat 3 meals every day
2. Eat bigger portions at mealtime
3. Eat an extra snack or two...before bed, between breakfast and lunch, between lunch and dinner...eat every few hours
4. Select higher calorie foods with a high nutrient value
 (not junk food, sweets, soda, etc.)
5. Eat enough protein to build muscle.
 (7gm/pound of body weight)

It is recommended to eat protein-rich foods and forget those expensive shakes!

6. Drink lots of milk and juice...they are high in calories
7. Consume extra calories to gain weight: (do the math)
 Women need approximately 22 calories/lb
 Men need approximately 23+ calories/lb
8. Strength Train: necessary to increase muscle mass
 8 to 10 exercises for the major muscle groups
 Three sets of 10 to 12 reps
 Three times per week

High Nutrient Food Ideas for Weight Gain

Peanut Butter	Trail Mix
Sandwiches	Smoothies
Fruit Yogurt	Milkshakes
Nuts	Beans & Bean Dishes
Cheese & Crackers	Pudding
Yogurt Raisins	Cookies & Milk
Ice Cream	Sunflower Seeds
Potato Soup	Instant Breakfast Drinks
Granola	Dried Fruits
Cottage Cheese	Pasta Dishes
Quiche	Frozen Yogurt

Registered dietitian, Liz Applegate, Ph.D., recommends the following daily to meet the increased protein needs for gaining weight:

5 to 6 oz. of lean meat
2 to 3 servings of soy products
2 to 3 servings of low-fat dairy
several servings of grains with legumes

Rather than spend money on expensive protein drinks, you can make your own for a lot less. The two recipes below can provide additional calories and protein to your diet!

High Protein Smoothie

Eat Smart, Play Hard, Liz Applegate, RD and Ph.D.
100% wholesome ingredients loaded with vitamins C & B6, antioxidants, potassium and fiber.

1 cup ice cubes
¾ cup pasteurized liquid egg substitute
¾ cup vanilla soy milk
1 cup frozen blueberries (or fruit of choice)
½ banana sliced
½ cup cranberry juice
1 Tbsp. honey

In a blender, combine the ice, egg substitute, milk, blueberries, banana, juice and honey on high for 30 seconds,

400 calories, 5g total fat, 25g protein, 65g carbohydrate, 5.5 g dietary fiber, 0mg cholesterol, and 489mg sodium

Weight Gain Formula

1 quart 2% milk
1 cup powdered milk
4 packets of instant breakfast drink

Mix together and refrigerate. Enjoy throughout the day!
1300 calories

What if you want or need to lose weight?

Before considering whether or not weight loss is an appropriate goal, it is recommended to get your body composition analyzed. Determining percentage of body fat or BMI will provide a guideline for goal setting with regards to weight loss. If your body fat percentage or BMI is in the healthy range but you are not satisfied with how you look, focus your goals on healthy eating and exercise rather than weight loss. Soon your body will respond with increased muscle tone. If you do in fact need to lose weight or reduce body fat, the recommendation is the same...focus your goals on healthy eating and exercise and the weight loss will follow! By redirecting your focus from dieting to healthy eating and exercise, you will improve your habits, your body, and your life!

Bottom Line: to lose weight you must consume fewer calories than you burn. Calorie counting is not necessary to achieve this goal. Following the Food Guide Pyramid recommendations for the number of servings from each of the food groups will help you focus on healthy eating and keep your calorie consumption in check. If necessary, revisit www.MyPyramid.gov to view your daily requirements for each of the food groups and record below.

Food Group	Your Daily # of Servings	Approximate Serving Size
Fruit		
Vegetables		
Dairy		
Carbohydrates		
Protein		
Healthy fats		
Water		

The pyramid emphasizes whole grains, fruits, vegetables, limiting fat and sugar, and eating appropriate portions of food. Review your food log to determine how well you have been meeting these recommendations. Begin making small changes to improve your eating habits. Don't try to change everything at once! Think of one or two bad habits and replace them with healthier habits. For example: replace pop with water; white bread with whole wheat; white rice with light brown rice; whole milk with 2% or skim milk; replace unhealthy snacks with fruit or nuts; chips with low-fat pretzels; add vegetables to pizza; add fruit to cereal; etc.

Work at meeting the Food Pyramid recommendations...don't eat more of one food group at the expense of another. Always strive to get the right amount of fruit and vegetables...they are low in calories and fat!

If you want to lose weight, improve physical fitness or change the shape of your body, **exercise is essential**! The Food Guide Pyramid also provides recommendations for physical activity for weight loss, improvement and/or maintenance of physical fitness. Refer to the Physical Activity section of the Pyramid to fill in the chart below.

Schedule in time for exercise! Make it a priority! When you are consistently exercising, weight management/loss is so much easier! Find a workout buddy...you will keep each other accountable and motivated. You will have to

Goal	Frequency Days/week	Duration Time/session
Weight Loss Fitness Gains		
Maintain Fitness Level		

"make time" to exercise. Everyone is busy but in order to achieve your goals and enhance your health, you have to exercise. Choose activities that you enjoy and use the time to connect with friends by exercising together.

Set a weight loss or exercise goal and visualize it! Tell your workout buddy, family or friends about the goal so they can encourage you along the way. Setting a goal will inspire and motivate you. A goal will help you plan the details along the way and overcome obstacles. Write your goal down along with positive statements of what you want to achieve and how it will make you feel. Put "reminders" around your house or room to motivate you...could be a picture or encouraging words.

Get rid of the excuses you have relied on in the past when you have tried to make a positive change. Accept responsibility and give yourself a chance to be successful. Recognize obstacles that have stood in the way of weight loss success in the past. Plan for ways to work around difficult situations so they do not interfere with your diet and exercise habits and goals. Learn to say no to activities or events that will set you up for failure! Your family and friends will be impressed by your new resolve to take control of your life and health. Positive thinking is a must! Stop negative self-talk and change it into positive statements that will re-enforce success. Believe in yourself! You can do anything that you decide to do! The power of your mind is amazing!

Convenient Snack Foods

Baby carrots
Celery
Broccoli
Apples
Oranges
Pears
Berries
Grapes

Raisins
Whole-Grain Bagels
Animal Crackers
Pretzels
Whole-Grain Crackers
Low-fat Yogurt
Nuts
Sunflower/Pumpkin Seeds

Helpful Healthy Eating Strategies

Eat a healthy breakfast...refer to page 31
Never skip a meal
Start your meals with soup
Reach for fruit and vegetables
Think small portions
Move before munching
Drink water before meals
Smell your food and enjoy every bite
Limit liquid calories
Eat heavy foods - ex. oranges vs. chips
Limit unhealthy choices
Be smart with sweets – eat small servings
Portion out foods...don't eat out of the bag
Don't totally deprive yourself of any food...just limit the amount
Drink 8-10 glasses of water daily
Enjoy your food...slow down and savor the food
Add new foods to your diet rather than focusing on the unhealthy foods you are trying to avoid
Plan ahead for meals and snacks
Avoid fast food and vending machines

"The key to good health and effective fat management is the frequency and amount of the <u>compromises</u> you allow in your daily diet."
Danna Demetre

Whether you need to gain weight, lose weight or maintain your weight...are there any suggestions from the lesson that <u>you could apply to your life</u>?

List three 'Helpful Healthy Eating" strategies that you will try to implement into your habits:

1.

2.

3.

43

Disease prevention...is it really possible?
YES!

You can seriously reduce your risk for Cardiovascular Disease, Diabetes, Stroke and some Cancers by a healthy lifestyle!
All of these diseases are influenced by...you guessed it, physical activity, a nutritious diet and weight management!

First, let's take a look at the role **obesity or overweight** plays in developing disease. According to the CDC (Center for Disease Control), obesity is the second leading cause of preventable deaths each year in the USA! The economic cost of obesity is $100 billion/year. Americans spend roughly $30 billion/year in attempts to lose weight! (We could have a huge discussion on the "diet industry") Obesity is a primary cause for cardiovascular disease, coronary heart disease, hypertension (high blood pressure), diabetes and some cancers. Obesity now fits the definition of a national epidemic. Eighty percent of Americans are heavier than they should be for good health. So while many Americans are not obese, the additional pounds also have a profound effect on their health!

Obesity is defined as a BMI ≥ 30 or a Body Fat % ≥ 30% for women.

Obesity contributes to:
→ *Coronary heart disease*
→ *High blood pressure*
→ *High cholesterol*
→ *Type 2 diabetes*
→ *Musculoskeletal disorders (arthritis, joint pain)*
→ *Sleep apnea and respiratory problems*
→ *Some cancers (endometrial, breast, prostate, colon)*
→ *Pregnancy complications*
→ *Poor female reproductive health*
→ *Bladder control problems*
→ *Psychological disorders (depression, eating disorders, distorted body image, low self-esteem)*

> Waist circumference is an indicator of good health. A healthy waist circumference for women is less than 33 inches and for men is less than 35 inches. For every 1-inch increase in waist circumference there is an increased risk for high blood pressure, high cholesterol, and metabolic syndrome.

What is metabolic syndrome?
Metabolic syndrome is a group of risk factors that increase the risk for heart disease, stroke, and type 2 diabetes. Up to 47 million US adults have metabolic syndrome and don't know it! The symptoms are silent for the most part until medical tests are done or problems start to creep up!

5 Risk Factors for Metabolic Syndrome
✓ *Abdominal obesity - Men ≥ 40 in. and Women ≥ 35 in.*
✓ *High blood pressure ≥ 130/85 mm Hg*
✓ *High blood sugar ≥ 100mg/dl*
✓ *High triglycerides (blood fatty acids) ≥ 150mg/dl*
✓ *Low levels of HDL (good cholesterol) - Men < 40mg/dl and Women < 50mg/dl*

> The American Heart Association recommends weight loss and increased physical activity to help reverse and prevent metabolic syndrome!

Type 2 Diabetes – *is also reaching epidemic proportions in the US and throughout the world! One out of every three children born in the year 2000 will develop diabetes. The number of people worldwide that had diabetes in 2000 was 151 million. If the current trend continues there will be 221 million by the year 2010 and 324 million by 2025! The economic cost of this epidemic is staggering! But even worse is the personal health cost for those who develop diabetes. When a person develops diabetes, either the body doesn't produce enough insulin or the cells ignore the insulin that is present in the blood stream. Either way, the body is unable to utilize the glucose or sugar that is present in the blood at the cell level for energy. As a result, the cells may be starved for energy and overtime high blood glucose levels can damage the eyes, kidneys, nerves or heart. Unfortunately, diabetes can go undetected for many years and may result in serious medical problems such as cardiovascular disease. Diabetes contributes to over 200,000 deaths in the US per year!*

Primary risk factors for Type 2 Diabetes:
- Obesity, excess fat
- Physical inactivity or sedentary lifestyle
- Poor eating habits
- Family history

Symptoms of Diabetes:
- Increased thirst
- Increased hunger
- Fatigue
- Increased urination
- Weight loss
- Blurred vision
- Sores that do not heal

Consequences of Diabetes:
*Loss of vision
*High cholesterol
*Heart disease
*Damage to organs
*Loss of limb/fingers/toes
*Poor quality of life
*Restricted diet
*Monitoring of blood glucose levels - DAILY
* Death

Diabetes Prevention
Lose Weight
Eat a Healthy Diet
Increase Physical Activity

High Blood Pressure – "Silent Killer"   *Normal Blood Pressure 120/80mmHg*

High Blood Pressure:
- increases the workload of the heart, which causes the heart to enlarge, and weakens the heart overtime
- increases the risk of stroke, heart attack, kidney failure and heart failure
- 72 million people in the US age 20 or older have high blood pressure
- 1 in 3 adults has high blood pressure, 1 in 4 twelve-year-olds has high blood pressure
- 30% of the people with high blood pressure don't know they have it
- 40% of African Americans have high blood pressure
- the death rate from high blood pressure increased 25% from 1994 to 2004

"Recently we lost a friend who was a 42-year-old mom to a massive heart attack…three months earlier she had experienced a stroke from high blood pressure! Take care of your body! Talk to your parents about taking care of themselves! Start today!"
                                                                                                                                                Betty Kern, MS, CSCS

Risk Factors for Heart Disease and Stroke according to the American Heart Association ♥

Uncontrollable Risk Factors
- Age
- Heredity and race

Other Major Risk Factors
- Tobacco smoking
- High blood cholesterol levels
- High blood pressure
- Physical inactivity
- Obesity and overweight – especially around the waist
- Diabetes – ⅔ to ¾ of people with diabetes die of some form of heart or blood vessel disease
- Birth control pills with smoking increase a woman's risk of heart disease
- Excessive alcohol intake
- Drug abuse
- Socioeconomic factors
- Sickle cell anemia
- Prior stroke
- Stress

Warning Signs for a Heart Attack

- Chest discomfort in the center of the chest that lasts more than a few minutes or goes away and comes back...could be pressure, squeezing, fullness or pain
- Discomfort in other areas of the upper body...pain or discomfort in one or both arms, the back, neck, jaw or stomach
- Shortness of breath
- Others...cold sweat, nausea or light headed

Warning Signs for a Stroke

- Sudden numbness/weakness of face, arms or legs, especially on one side
- Sudden confusion, trouble speaking or understanding
- Sudden trouble seeing
- Sudden trouble walking, dizziness, loss of balance or coordination
- Sudden, severe headache
- DON'T DELAY...CALL 911...Clot busting drugs administered within 3 hours of a stroke can reduce long-term disability for most strokes

Warning Signs for Cardiac Arrest

- Cardiac arrest strikes immediately without warning
- Sudden loss of responsiveness
- No normal breathing → call 911 immediately and begin CPR!

> Heart attack, stroke, and cardiac arrest can happen to anyone at any age! If you, a friend or family member experience any of these symptoms, get help immediately! Immediate medical care can stop the damage that is occurring to your heart, brain and body!

Cancer - "We need to think of cancer as the product of many long-term influences, not as something that just happens."

Dr. Walter J. Willet, Professor of Epidemiology and Nutrition at the Harvard School of Public Health

President Richard Nixon declared the war on cancer more than 35 years ago. Although once thought to be a mysterious disease, research has uncovered links between certain cancers and various lifestyle choices. Unbelievable progress has been made in the prevention and treatment of cancer. Early detection of cancer is of the utmost importance! "If all cancers were detected at stage 1 or 2, current therapies could cure almost every case," says Carolyn D. Runowicz, MD. Robert A. Smith, Ph D adds, "Presently, nothing in our armamentarium is more effective than finding a localized tumor before it has spread."

The American Cancer Society has issued a Complete Guide to Cancer Prevention, which details healthy lifestyle habits to follow for cancer prevention. Below is a summary of that report:

> - **Maintain a healthy weight throughout life by balancing caloric intake with physical activity**. If currently overweight, take the necessary steps to achieve and maintain a healthy weight.
> - **Adopt a physically active lifestyle by exercising at least 30 minutes a day for adults and 60 minutes a day for children and adolescents**. Exercises should be moderate (require the effort of a brisk walk) to vigorous (increase heart rate, breathing rate and causes sweating). For optimal cancer prevention, adults should aim for 45 to 60 minutes of exercise most days of the week.
> - Exercise has proven to be a key cancer fighter!
> - **Eat a healthy diet emphasizing fruit and vegetables (5+ servings daily), whole grains, and lean meat**. Limit consumption of processed grains, processed meats, red meat, saturated fat, Trans fat, sugary and processed baked goods and snacks. Eat appropriate sized portions of foods and beverages to help maintain a healthy weight.
> - Alcohol consumption has been linked to several types of cancer. **It is recommended to abstain from alcohol** or to at least limit the amount of alcohol to no more than one drink per day for women and no more than two drinks per day for men. "Saving" up your allotted drinks for the week and consuming them all on the weekend is not a good choice for maintaining good health.
> - **Do not use any tobacco products**. Tobacco raises the risk of cancers of the mouth, nasal passages, larynx, throat, esophagus, stomach, liver, pancreas, kidney, bladder and cervix. The Center for Disease Control reports that at least 30% of all cancer deaths are due to smoking. It is never too late to quit smoking. Ten years after a person quits smoking, his/her risk of developing lung cancer is one-half that of someone who continued smoking.
> - Several types of cancer are linked with excess weight or obesity:

*breast	*colon	*endometrial (uterine)	*esophagus	*kidney	*cervix
*gallbladder	*Hodgkin lymphoma	*ovarian	*pancreas	*thyroid	*prostate (aggressive forms)

> - Physical activity may reduce the risk of several types of cancer: breast, colon, uterine, and prostate. Plus, exercise will aid in maintaining appropriate weight and reduce the risk of the cancers listed above.

Skin Cancer – is the most common of all cancer types according to the American Cancer Society. More than 1 million skin cancers are diagnosed each year in the USA! That is more than all of the diagnosed cases of prostate, breast, lung, colon, uterine, ovarian, and pancreas cancers combined each year. The good news is that there is a lot you can do to protect yourself from developing skin cancer.

Two types of skin cancer: Non-melanoma and Melanoma.

Non-melanoma –
- most common type
- mainly found on head and neck
- occurrence is related to amount of sun exposure over a lifetime
- less likely to be fatal…but still requires treatment

Melanoma – can occur anywhere on the body
- trunk is most common in men
- legs are most common in women
- curable in early stages
- if left untreated, will spread to other parts of the body
- late detection makes it difficult to treat

> Slip! Slop! Slap!…and Wrap!
> -for skin protection
> Slip on a shirt!
> Slop on sunscreen!
> Slap on a hat!
> Wrap on sunglasses!
> American Cancer society

> Tanning beds are dangerous because they give off UVA & UVB rays, which contribute to skin damage and skin cancer. Is the tan really worth the risk?

Ultraviolet (UV) Radiation – a form of invisible energy given off by the sun
UVA Rays: help age skin; causes some damage to cells' DNA; linked to long-term skin damage such as wrinkles; play a role in skin cancers
UVB Rays: mainly responsible for direct damage to cells' DNA; rays that cause sunburn; thought to cause most skin cancers
Too much sun can cause skin cancer, aged skin, wrinkles, loss of skin elasticity, dark patches, pre-cancerous skin changes including dry, scaly, rough-textured patches.

Risk Factors for Skin Cancer:

*everyone's skin & eyes can be damaged by the sun
*tanning is a form of skin damage
*having a lot of moles
*live or vacation at high altitudes or in tropical locations
*auto-immune disease
*various medications…read info packet

*people with light skin are at a greater risk
*sunburns increase risk of skin cancer
*previous skin cancer
*spending a lot of time outdoors
*organ transplants
*birth control pills

Prevention: Skin Exams…self-exam monthly and physician exam at yearly check-up! See a doctor for any 'trouble spots' or changes in the skin. Short periods of time in the sunlight help your body make vitamin D and can be important for good health. However, too much sunlight can be harmful. Sun exposure adds up day after day, year after year…it happens every time you are in the sun. Apply sunscreen with an SPF of 15 or higher for protection. Apply generously to dry skin 20 to 30 minutes before going outside. Reapply every two hours. Limit exposure between 10am and 4pm.

> "If we are watching our weight, working regular physical activity into our daily life and eating a healthy balance of foods, we could prevent 1/3 of cancers. Extra weight is not dead weight. It's an active metabolic tissue that produces substances that promote the development of cancer."
> Karen Collins
> Nutrition Advisor at American Institute for Cancer Research

Osteoporosis

<u>Osteoporosis</u> - is a disease of bone thinning and deterioration that leads to fragile bones and increases the risk of fracture.

Osteoporosis is a silent disease...... most people do not realize that their bones are thinning until a fracture occurs.

According to the U.S. Surgeon General in 2004:

*Osteoporosis affects approximately **25 million Americans.**

***80% of those affected are WOMEN!**

***34 Million Americans** are at risk with low bone mass or "osteopenia."

***Osteoporosis causes 1.5 million fractures per year.**

-1/2 million are thoracic and lumbar vertebrae and result in a deformed, hunched posture that contributes to back pain and poor self-image.

-1/4 million are fractures of the hip and result in 15-20% higher death rates and increased disability.

*1 out of every 2 women over age 50 will have an osteoporosis related fracture in their lifetime, with risks increasing with age.

*The direct financial expenditures are approximately $18 billion per year.

*Osteoporosis can occur in men; 6% of white men over age 50 will suffer a hip fracture.

***The bone most vulnerable to osteoporosis is trabecular bone, which is located in the spine and hip.**

Bone mass is built in the body throughout childhood and young adulthood. Bone mass peaks between ages 25 and 30. Around age 35 bone mass begins to decline. IT IS CRUCIAL FOR CHILDREN, ADOLESCENTS, TEENS, AND YOUNG ADULTS TO DO EVERYTHING THEY CAN TO MAXIMIZE THEIR PEAK BONE MASS!! Many factors affect the peak bone mass that can be attained by an individual. Proper nutrition, exercise and healthy habits can maximize peak bone mass and prevent bone loss as one ages.

"A negative balance of only 50-100 mg of calcium per day over a long period of time is sufficient to produce osteoporosis," cautions the Surgeon General.

Calcium

<u>Why do you need calcium?</u>

1. **Calcium promotes strong teeth and bones.**

Calcium is continually deposited in multiplying bone cells. The stronger the bone development during childhood and adolescence, the healthier those bones will be in adulthood. Bone grows rapidly during the teen years so a large supply of calcium is essential for bone health.

2. **Calcium helps muscles.** If muscles are not supplied with enough calcium, they can cramp and fail, even the heart muscle.

3. **Calcium helps nerves.** Nerve impulses, the transmission of information along the nerve fibers, will not function properly without the right amount of calcium.

Calcium is one of the most vital minerals for optimal functioning of your entire body.

<u>How does calcium work?</u>

The body has an amazing system for keeping the concentration of minerals, including calcium, in the blood and tissues just right. This system is needed because if the concentration of calcium is too high or too low in the blood, certain organs will fail to function. Maintenance of this concentration is performed through the check-points in the intestines and bones. When there is insufficient calcium in the diet, the body may borrow what it needs from the bones. This will work for a while but you can imagine the problem for the bones if this practice continues. The parathyroid hormone oversees all this calcium activity in the body. When calcium levels fall, this hormone stimulates the release of vitamin D to increase absorption of calcium from the intestines and to release calcium from the bone bank until a proper balance is restored.

<u>Factors Affecting Calcium Absorption</u>

*Stress from tension and worry can decrease calcium absorption.

*Calcium is best absorbed when taken in smaller amounts, more frequently and with meals.

***Dairy products are a rich source of calcium and lactose which help facilitate calcium absorption.**

***Vitamin D improves the absorption of calcium.**

*The presence of estrogen facilitates calcium absorption.

*"Couch-potatoism", or lack of exercise, may contribute, as much or more, to osteoporosis than lack of calcium.

*SOFT DRINKS THAT CONTAIN CITRIC AND PHOSPHORIC ACID CAN DECREASE THE ABSORPTION OF CALCIUM......
A 12-ONCE COLA MAY ROB THE BODY OF 100MG OF CALCIUM!!

Calcium and Vitamin D Requirements

Age	Calcium (milligrams per day)	Vitamin D (IU per day)
Adolescents/Young Adults (11-24 years old)	1200-1500 mg 3-4 SERVINGS A DAY!	200 IU
Pregnant/Lactating Women	1200-1500 mg	200 IU
Women (25-50 years old)	1000 mg	200 IU

Best Dairy Sources of Calcium:

1 cup nonfat plain yogurt - 450mg
1 cup nonfat fruit yogurt - 400 mg
parmesan cheese (1 oz) - 336mg

low fat plain yogurt - 400mg
1 cup ice cream - 200mg
1 cup low fat milk - 300mg

1 oz cheddar cheese - 200 mg
1 cup cottage cheese - 155 mg
romano cheese (1oz) - 302 mg

Best Non-Dairy Sources of Calcium:

sesame seeds 1 oz – 280mg
collards ½ cup – 180mg
Spinach ½ cup – 136mg
almonds 1 oz – 80mg
beans ½ cup – 75mg

sardines 3oz – 371 mg
tofu 3 oz – 190mg
rhubarb ½ cup – 174mg
figs (5) – 135mg
broccoli ½ cup – 47mg

orange juice 1 cup – 300mg
Salmon 3 oz – 180mg
molasses 1Tbsp – 172m
soybean nuts ¼ cup – 116mg
orange 1 med – 50mg

Calcium from foods is the best option for maintaining bone health and integrity as well as overall health. However, if calcium intake from the diet is inadequate, calcium supplements can be helpful for some individuals to meet their calcium requirements.

Other Nutrients important to bone health:

1. **Vitamin D**
   - Obtained mostly from sunlight
   - People who live in the north need to increase vitamin D intake from fall to spring

2. **Vitamin K -**
   "The Green Vitamin"
   - Crucial in the production of "the bone matrix" which is the protein called osteocalcin. If deficient in vitamin K, the body doesn't make as much bone matrix and therefore, produces less bone.

3. **Protein -**
   - If a person is taking calcium and vitamin K supplements and is getting sufficient calcium to meet his/her daily requirements, protein aids in bone production.
   - However, if calcium and vitamin D intakes are insufficient, protein actually contributes to accelerated loss of calcium from the body, thereby leading to less bone production.

4. **Potassium -**
   - A study showed that the more potassium that people ingested, the less calcium they excreted - *The Nutrition Acton Health Letter* April 2005.
   - Ingest potassium naturally through fruits and vegetables....it can be lethal as a supplement.

5. **Fruits & Veggies -**
   - Americans eat more foods that produce acid than alkali. Grains (breads, pasta, rice and baked goods) and protein foods (meat, poultry and seafood) generate acid residues in the body. The body must neutralize this extra acid so it uses bone because it is our biggest reservoir of alkali in the body. The body breaks down bone, as well as, muscle to help neutralize extra acid according to the Nutrition Action Health Letter, April 2005. To avoid the breakdown of bone and muscle and to keep a neutral system, eat more fruits and vegetables. The digestion of fruits and vegetables produces alkali which helps balance the system.

6. **Vitamin A -**
   - Too much vitamin A can be a problem with calcium absorption.
   - Choose a multivitamin with no more than 2,000 to 3,000 IU of vitamin A from retinol.

Exercise

"Strain is good. The body constantly monitors how much strain muscles put on bones. More strain signals the body to build bone. Less strain sends a message to break down bone."   Nutrition Action Health Letter April 2005

Physical Activity and maintaining a healthy weight are important throughout life for bone health!
 Weight bearing exercises help build bone mass. Examples include: running, walking, hiking, dancing, tennis, gardening, aerobics, golf, weight training, etc..

In summary, to help build and maintain a healthy bone mass, adhere to the following recommendations:

*meet calcium and vitamin D recommendations
*limit alcohol use
*be physically active
*do not smoke
*maintain a healthy weight

How are you doing?

Are you getting enough calcium in your diet?

How could you consume more calcium?

Are you exercising enough to help build healthy bones?

How could you incorporate more activity into your day?

Do you have any unhealthy "habits" that may negatively affect your bone health?

Disease Prevention Questions/Assignment

Name _____

1. Obesity is the primary cause of what diseases?

2. Define obesity with regards to BMI and percentage of body fat for men and women.

3. Do you think the teens in America understand the role that being overweight or obese plays in determining their current health status and their future health?

4. Propose an effective plan to inform the young adult and teen population of the importance of weight control for prevention of disease.

5. After discussing the major diseases that affect Americans (diabetes, obesity, heart disease, high blood pressure, cancer), what are the two most important lifestyle habits that you can adopt that positively influences all of these disease states?

6. Why do so many Americans ignore the advice of doctors and nutritionists concerning diet and exercise?

7. Genetics or family history often increases the risk of developing diabetes, heart disease, high blood pressure, and cancer. It is important for you to know your family history with respect to these diseases and others. Have you questioned your family or do you know your family history for these diseases?

8. Do you have any habits that you should change in order to positively affect your health and reduce your risk of developing these disease states?

10. Compose a list of healthy habits that you will adopt that could alter your risk factors for developing life-threatening diseases.

Personal Health

If you ask 100 women if they are happy with their breasts, 95 will probably answer no.
Some will say they are too small and others will say they are too large!
Whether you are satisfied or not...it is very important to be concerned about your breast health!
You are never too young to be concerned about taking good care of your body!

A regular yearly physical is important for prevention of disease and catching problems while they are still manageable and/or treatable.

A. Breast Cancer - prevention & lifestyle choices

Does healthy eating and regular exercise really contribute to breast cancer prevention?
The evidence says YES!

There are always risks you cannot control...such as your age and genetics. But there are lifestyle choices that appear to reduce the risk of developing breast cancer. There is no guarantee that you will not develop breast cancer but these strategies will help to decrease your risk. Adopting a healthy lifestyle in your teens will help you prevent or delay many diseases that are associated with poor habits.

According to a Mayo Clinic article, the following strategies will help prevent breast cancer.

- ❖ **Maintain a healthy weight** – there is a clear link between obesity and breast cancer
- ❖ **Stay physically active** – regular exercise will help you maintain a healthy weight and reduce the risk for developing breast cancer. Thirty minutes of exercise is recommended for most days of the week with one or two days at sixty plus minutes. It is important for some of the exercise to be done at a higher intensity to help burn more calories and fat. Try to include power walking, jogging or aerobics in your exercise plan.
- ❖ **Limit alcohol** – there is a strong link between alcohol consumption and breast cancer. It is recommended to limit alcohol to less than one drink per day or to avoid alcohol completely.
- ❖ **Limit the amount of unhealthy fat in your diet** – limit fat to less than 35% of your daily calories and restrict foods high in saturated and trans fat. Eat more fruits and vegetables and less processed foods. When you do eat processed foods, read the label and avoid the bad fats (listed page 22)!

B. Self-Exam

Did you know...that women who perform regular breast self-exams find 90% of all breast lumps? Even though you are a teen it is still important to examine your breasts regularly to see if any unusual changes have occurred. Detecting breast cancer early is the most effective way to fight it! Although 80% of all breast lumps are not cancerous, once you have discovered a lump or change in the breasts a doctor should evaluate it immediately. Developing the habit of regular monthly self-exams during your teen years will help you continue the habit and protect your health as an adult. Doctors recommend a clinical breast exam by a health professional every three years until you are 40. After age 40 you should have a mammogram and a clinical breast exam each year. Ask your mom, aunts, grandmas and other adult women in your life if they have had a mammogram this year!

According to the experts, the best time to do a self-exam is three to five days after your menstrual period ends each month.

The following steps for self-breast exam were taken from the WebMD and the Mayo Clinic web sites.

In the mirror:

1. Stand in front of a mirror undressed from the waist up. Look closely at your breasts. With your arms relaxed by your sides, look for any changes in size, shape or position, puckering, dimpling or changes in symmetry. Most women's breasts are not exactly the same in size or shape so don't be alarmed if yours are not either. Also look for any changes in the skin color or sores. Inspect your nipples to see if there are any changes...turned in or leaking fluid.

2. Place your hands on your hips and press down firmly to tighten your chest muscles. Turn from side to side to also inspect the outer part of the breast.

3. Bend forward toward the mirror and roll your shoulders and elbows forward to tighten your chest muscles this way. Look for any changes in the shape of your breasts.

4. Clasp your hands behind your head and press your hands together. Turn from side to side to inspect the outer part of the breasts again. Remember to check the area under your breasts. You may need to lift your breasts with your hand to see this area clearly.

In the shower:

5. Lather your fingers and breasts with soap to help your fingers glide more smoothly over your wet skin. To check for any lumps or thickening under your arm, place your left hand on your hip and reach with your right hand to feel in the left armpit...this is an area where a lot of tumors occur. Check it carefully! Repeat on the other side.

6. Check above and below your collarbone for lumps or thickenings on both sides.

7. The clock pattern:
   - visualize your breast as the face of a clock
   - place your left hand behind your head and examine your left breast with your right hand
   - place your right hand at 12 o'clock – at the very top of your breast
   - press the pads of your three middle fingers firmly on your breast in a slight circling, massaging motion
   - move your hand down to 1 o'clock, then 2 o'clock and so on all the way around
   - continue in the same pattern, moving your hand in smaller circles toward your nipple
   - check the tissue under the nipple by gently pressing it inward...it should move easily
   - place your right hand behind your head and repeat the exam on the right breast using your left hand
   - be sure to examine the whole breast area including the under arm area
   - if you detect ANY CHANGES, SEE YOUR DOCTOR IMMEDIATELY for an evaluation

Breast changes that should be checked by a doctor include:

   - an area that is different from any other area on the breast
   - a lump or thickening in or near the breast or in the underarm that lasts through your period
   - a change in the shape or contour of the breast...obviously some of you may still be developing but if something just doesn't look the same or right...get it checked out
   - a mass or lump...it could be as small as a pea
   - a marble-like area under the skin...kind of like dimples
   - a change in the feel or appearance of the skin on the breast or nipple
   - bloody or clear fluid leaking from the nipple
   - redness of the skin on the breast or nipple

The most important advice is...if you feel something is wrong...go with your feelings and get checked by a doctor. You may even want to get more than one opinion if you are not satisfied with the first doctor's evaluation.

You know your body best!

Sports Bras

Did you know that the first "jog bra" was made from two jock straps sewn together?
Aren't we thankful there have been some changes in the sports bra industry since the 1970s?

Why do you need a sports bra?

Although exercise will help prevent breasts from sagging, some sagging will occur over time. The reason is that the breasts have no muscle in them that you can actually tone. Developing the muscles under the breast help with appearance but breast tissue needs to be supported and protected especially during exercise and sport activities. The ligaments that attach the breasts to the chest are delicate and if not supported will break down from the constant motion of exercise. Wearing a sports bra is necessary for all exercise and sport activities regardless of the size of your breasts. Larger breasted women need additional support and should purchase bras designed specifically for them.

Different sports exert different stresses on your body and breasts. The "sport impact level" may help you determine the type of sports bra to purchase. Companies have designed bras for various levels of stress or impact. Obviously the higher the impact or stress of the activity, the more support is needed. Examples of moderate stress activities: weight training, walking, cycling, snow skiing, and in-line skating. Medium stress activities include: rowing, golf, tennis, martial arts, step aerobics, lacrosse, stair climbing, and field hockey. High stress activities include: basketball, softball, volleyball, running, horseback riding, racquetball, etc. If you are involved in a high impact activity, you need to wear a good sports bra.

Sports bras should be replaced at least every six months if worn regularly to maintain proper support during exercise. You should wash the sports bra after each time you wear it!

There are various types of sports bras made from a wide range of fabrics and designs. The moisture-wicking fabrics are comfortable and help keep you cool and dry during exercise. You may want to experiment with different styles and fabrics to determine your preference. The racer back or traditional sports bra is said to give the most support to larger breasted women. It is actually a good design for all women because it affords greater freedom of movement. The most important advice is to always wear a sports bra when exercising to protect breast tissue from breaking down. Once the damage is done it is almost impossible to reverse it!

Will exercise affect your breast size?

Yes...but don't freak out!
With a combination of the right exercises and some good advice you can minimize breast loss.
Shapely arms, abs and legs will get you noticed as well.

<u>Muscle & Fitness Hers</u> gives you three rules every woman should follow no matter what:
1. **Never train (especially running) without a sports bra.**
2. **Don't lose weight too quickly**...no more than 1 – 2 pounds per week...more will cause your body to pull fat stores from all fat reserves including your breasts!
3. **Tolerate some fat**...a few pounds can make a real difference for your breast size

Exercise can help...developing the muscles underneath the breasts will push the breast tissue outward...adding both size and definition to the area. Exercise will also help improve your posture, which will help create the appearance of a larger chest. Don't waste your money on creams or pills to help enhance your breast size. With some hard work in the gym you can shape and enhance your chest with the right exercises.

The workout from <u>Muscle and Fitness Hers</u> to help enhance your chest:
Perform each pair of exercises alternating between a & b with 3 to 4 sets of 10 reps per exercise then move on to the next pair.

1a. Dumbbell Flies

2a. Chest press w/DB or bands

3a. Push-ups

1b. YTI
Lie face down on a bench lift arms at the three different angles and repeat.

2b. Cable Crossovers

3b Dumbbell Row

Personal Health...con't

Gynecologist Visits

A gynecologist is a doctor who specializes in women's reproductive health. So a gynecologist is concerned about the health of your female organs including breasts, ovaries, fallopian tubes, vagina, uterus, cervix, etc. You may be wondering why this should concern a teenage girl. Well...the reproductive system is one of the most delicate, easily damaged systems of the body. Damage to your reproductive system in your teens caused by injury or disease can affect the health of this system for the rest of your life. Therefore, taking good care of every aspect of your health is important even in your teens. Remember... good hygiene is extremely important! Shower/bathe and change underwear everyday!

When do you need to see the gynecologist?

It is recommended for girls between the ages of thirteen and fifteen to schedule a visit to the gynecologist. If you are sexually active in any way...vaginal sex, anal sex, oral sex or are intimate sexually even without intercourse...you need to see a gynecologist. If you have lower stomach pain, fever and a vaginal discharge that is yellow, gray or green with a strong smell, you should schedule a visit to the gynecologist. Between periods it is normal to have clear or whitish fluid or discharge coming from the vagina...it should not itch, burn or smell bad.

Why should you go to the gynecologist?

Establishing a doctor-patient relationship with a gynecologist in your teens can help you begin healthy lifestyle habits in the area of sexual health. Your doctor will help you understand how your body works, establish what is normal for you, find problems early so they can be effectively treated, discuss with you why it is healthier for teenagers not to have sex, explain how to protect yourself if you do have sex, and help you prepare for healthy relationships and future pregnancies.

What will happen at a gynecologist visit?

At your first exam you can expect the doctor to do a general physical exam which includes height, weight and blood pressure.
The doctor should ask you questions about your general health as well as specific questions concerning your menstrual periods, sexual activity and family history. It is extremely important for you to be open and honest when answering the doctor's questions. Now is the time for you to ask the doctor questions about anything that may be concerning you about your health: cramps/problems with your period, acne, weight issues, sleep issues, STDs, depression, etc. Confidentiality is important to your doctor concerning your health. If you are worried about what might be shared with your parents, talk with the doctor about this issue first. There are certain kinds of information that the doctor must share with your parents and other information that can be kept confidential. The doctor will also perform a breast exam to check for lumps in the breast. If you have not been sexually active, then a pelvic exam is not necessary at this time unless you are having certain problems. If you have been sexually active, the doctor will do a pelvic exam to check your reproductive organs. This includes an external and internal exam. A Pap test will also be taken if you have been sexually active to check for abnormal cells on your cervix that could lead to cervical cancer. If you have been sexually active (even once), ask the doctor to test you for sexually transmitted infections or disease (STIs & STDs).

Whether you think about STDs, STIs, HPV, AIDS, etc. or not...you should!

Did you know
- ...STDs are the most common infectious diseases in the USA!
- ...there are more than 25 different STDs
- ...STDs can be contracted through any type of sexual contact (vaginal, oral or anal sex and intimate sexual contact)
- ...most STDs have no symptoms at first
- ...most STDs are not curable...symptoms are only "managed"
- ...STDs affect emotional and physical health
- ...STDs can cause infertility
- ...only way to be sure whether or not you are infected is to be tested by a doctor
- ...two-thirds of all STDs occur in people younger than age 25
- ...one out of four teens is infected with the HPV virus which causes genital warts and cervical cancer...no visual symptoms initially
- ...even if you are treated for an STD, you can get it back by having sex with someone who is infected
- ...condoms offer protection against most STDs if used correctly...they must be put on before any sexual contact!
- ...condoms do not protect against skin to skin contact in the genital area...so it is still possible to spread an STD through genital contact without intercourse!

STD Tests
- ...if you have been sexually active, it is important to be tested...many STDs have no symptoms in the early stages of infection
- ...some STDs can be treated if found early enough
- ...the doctor will examine your skin, throat and genital area including your vagina and cervix for sores, growths or skin rashes
- ...a sample of fluid or tissue from the skin, genital, vaginal or anal areas will be tested as well as blood and urine

If you think you have an STD...talk to your parents or an adult you can trust
- **...see a doctor**...get treatment right away
- ...follow the doctor's instructions including finishing all medications prescribed
- ...avoid all sexual contact during treatment for an STD...you can still pass it on to others at this time
- ...tell your partner...you both should be tested!
- ...follow up with check-ups and STD tests as recommended by your doctor

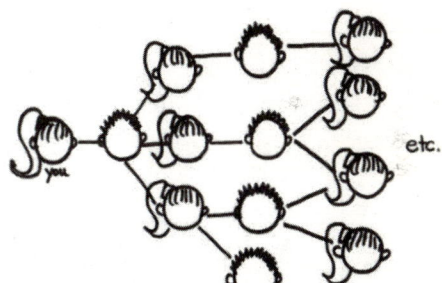

One partner can potentially expose you to a countless number of individuals' sexual health/disease through his past & present partners!

<u>**THE ONLY TRULY "SAFE" OPTION IS ABSTINENCE...YOU WILL NOT GET AN STD IF YOU ARE NOT SEXUALLY INTIMATE OR ACTIVE!**</u>

The emotional impact of being sexually active before marriage is huge! One teen girl said she felt like she was giving away little pieces of herself every time she had sex! Sex is not what will make a relationship work! **Think about your goals in life and how being sexually active could affect them!**

First Quarter

Journal Pages

Complete the following pages by recording your nutrition and exercise habits. Please complete questions as they appear on various pages.

Be honest about your habits. The purpose of the journal is to help you see a realistic picture of your habits and track the positive changes you make!

Every step takes you a little closer to your goal!

Week 1

Monday water ☐☐☐☐☐☐☐☐
Breakfast: _____ dairy ☐☐☐☐☐
_____ veggies ☐☐☐☐☐
Lunch: _____ fruit ☐☐☐☐☐
_____ protein ☐☐☐☐
Snack: _____ carbs ☐☐☐☐☐
Dinner: _____ healthy fats ☐☐☐☐
_____ soft drinks____ coffee____
_____ Sleep # hours _____
Snack: _____ Vitamins Yes ☐   No ☐
Discretionary Calories:
  Fast food ☐☐☐☐☐   Sweets ☐☐☐☐☐
  Junk food ☐☐☐☐☐   Other ☐☐☐☐☐

Tuesday water ☐☐☐☐☐☐☐☐
Breakfast: _____ dairy ☐☐☐☐☐
_____ veggies ☐☐☐☐☐
Lunch: _____ fruit ☐☐☐☐☐
_____ protein ☐☐☐☐
Snack: _____ carbs ☐☐☐☐☐
Dinner: _____ healthy fats ☐☐☐☐
_____ soft drinks____ coffee____
_____ Sleep # hours _____
Snack: _____ Vitamins Yes ☐   No ☐
Discretionary Calories:
  Fast food ☐☐☐☐☐   Sweets ☐☐☐☐☐
  Junk food ☐☐☐☐☐   Other ☐☐☐☐☐

"In one study, overweight people who kept a food journal for a year lost 41½ pounds, compared with just 17 pounds for those who didn't keep track."
PREVENTION, December 2006

Wednesday water ☐☐☐☐☐☐☐☐
Breakfast: _____ dairy ☐☐☐☐☐
_____ veggies ☐☐☐☐☐
Lunch: _____ fruit ☐☐☐☐☐
_____ protein ☐☐☐☐
Snack: _____ carbs ☐☐☐☐☐
Dinner: _____ healthy fats ☐☐☐☐
_____ soft drinks____ coffee____
_____ Sleep # hours _____
Snack: _____ Vitamins Yes ☐   No ☐
Discretionary Calories:
  Fast food ☐☐☐☐☐   Sweets ☐☐☐☐☐
  Junk food ☐☐☐☐☐   Other ☐☐☐☐☐

Thursday water ☐☐☐☐☐☐☐☐
Breakfast: _____ dairy ☐☐☐☐☐
_____ veggies ☐☐☐☐☐
Lunch: _____ fruit ☐☐☐☐☐
_____ protein ☐☐☐☐
Snack: _____ carbs ☐☐☐☐☐
Dinner: _____ healthy fats ☐☐☐☐
_____ soft drinks____ coffee____
_____ Sleep # hours _____
Snack: _____ Vitamins Yes ☐   No ☐
Discretionary Calories:
  Fast food ☐☐☐☐☐   Sweets ☐☐☐☐☐
  Junk food ☐☐☐☐☐   Other ☐☐☐☐☐

Friday water ☐☐☐☐☐☐☐☐
Breakfast: _____ dairy ☐☐☐☐☐
_____ veggies ☐☐☐☐☐
Lunch: _____ fruit ☐☐☐☐☐
_____ protein ☐☐☐☐
Snack: _____ carbs ☐☐☐☐☐
Dinner: _____ healthy fats ☐☐☐☐
_____ soft drinks____ coffee____
_____ Sleep # hours _____
Snack: _____ Vitamins Yes ☐   No ☐
Discretionary Calories:
  Fast food ☐☐☐☐☐   Sweets ☐☐☐☐☐
  Junk food ☐☐☐☐☐   Other ☐☐☐☐☐

"Those who are victorious plan effectively and change decisively."
Sun Tzu

Saturday water ☐☐☐☐☐☐☐☐
Breakfast: _____ dairy ☐☐☐☐☐
_____ veggies ☐☐☐☐☐
Lunch: _____ fruit ☐☐☐☐☐
_____ protein ☐☐☐☐
Snack: _____ carbs ☐☐☐☐☐
Dinner: _____ healthy fats ☐☐☐☐
_____ soft drinks____ coffee____
_____ Sleep # hours _____
Snack: _____ Vitamins Yes ☐   No ☐
Discretionary Calories:
  Fast food ☐☐☐☐☐   Sweets ☐☐☐☐☐
  Junk food ☐☐☐☐☐   Other ☐☐☐☐☐

Sunday water ☐☐☐☐☐☐☐☐
Breakfast: _____ dairy ☐☐☐☐☐
_____ veggies ☐☐☐☐☐
Lunch: _____ fruit ☐☐☐☐☐
_____ protein ☐☐☐☐
Snack: _____ carbs ☐☐☐☐☐
Dinner: _____ healthy fats ☐☐☐☐
_____ soft drinks____ coffee____
_____ Sleep # hours _____
Snack: _____ Vitamins Yes ☐   No ☐
Discretionary Calories:
  Fast food ☐☐☐☐☐   Sweets ☐☐☐☐☐
  Junk food ☐☐☐☐☐   Other ☐☐☐☐☐

FITNESS TESTING RESULTS

Test	
Height	
Weight	
BMI	
% Body Fat	
Resting Heart Rate	
Aerobic Test	
Waist Circumference	

Week #1

Name_____

Strength Training Log

Exercises	Date	Date	Exercises	Date	Date
Chest			Arms		
Back			Core		
Shoulders			Legs/Glutes		

Cardio Log

	Cardio Exercise	# Mins	Intensity Level	# Miles
Mon				
Tue				
Wed				
Thur				
Fri				
Sat				
Sun				
	Total Minutes ____		Total Miles ____	

Nutrition Goal for this week:

_____

Exercise Goal for this week:

_____

List your goals for fitness testing:

Weight	BMI	% Body fat	Resting Heart Rate	Aerobic Test	Waist			

Week 2

Monday water ☐ ☐ ☐ ☐ ☐ ☐ ☐ ☐
Breakfast: _____   dairy ☐ ☐ ☐ ☐ ☐ ☐
_____   veggies ☐ ☐ ☐ ☐ ☐ ☐
Lunch: _____   fruit ☐ ☐ ☐ ☐ ☐
_____   protein ☐ ☐ ☐ ☐ ☐
Snack: _____   carbs ☐ ☐ ☐ ☐ ☐ ☐
Dinner: _____   healthy fats ☐ ☐ ☐ ☐ ☐
_____   soft drinks____ coffee____
_____   Sleep # hours _____
Snack: _____   Vitamins Yes ☐   No ☐

Discretionary Calories:
Fast food ☐ ☐ ☐ ☐   Sweets ☐ ☐ ☐ ☐ ☐
Junk food ☐ ☐ ☐ ☐   Other ☐ ☐ ☐ ☐ ☐

Tuesday water ☐ ☐ ☐ ☐ ☐ ☐ ☐ ☐
Breakfast: _____   dairy ☐ ☐ ☐ ☐ ☐ ☐
_____   veggies ☐ ☐ ☐ ☐ ☐ ☐
Lunch: _____   fruit ☐ ☐ ☐ ☐ ☐ ☐
_____   protein ☐ ☐ ☐ ☐ ☐
Snack: _____   carbs ☐ ☐ ☐ ☐ ☐ ☐
Dinner: _____   healthy fats ☐ ☐ ☐ ☐ ☐
_____   soft drinks____ coffee____
_____   Sleep # hours _____
Snack: _____   Vitamins Yes ☐   No

Discretionary Calories:
Fast food ☐ ☐ ☐ ☐   Sweets ☐ ☐ ☐ ☐ ☐
Junk food ☐ ☐ ☐ ☐   Other ☐ ☐ ☐ ☐ ☐

Did you know…
Water is the #1 trigger of daytime fatigue! A drop of only 2% in body water can trigger fuzzy short-term memory, trouble with basic math, and difficulty focusing when reading! One glass of water can shut down midnight hunger pangs for almost 100% of dieters! Mild dehydration can slow down one's metabolism as much as 3%… you know what that means!

Wednesday water ☐ ☐ ☐ ☐ ☐ ☐ ☐ ☐
Breakfast: _____   dairy ☐ ☐ ☐ ☐ ☐ ☐
_____   veggies ☐ ☐ ☐ ☐ ☐
Lunch: _____   fruit ☐ ☐ ☐ ☐ ☐
_____   protein ☐ ☐ ☐ ☐
Snack: _____   carbs ☐ ☐ ☐ ☐ ☐
Dinner: _____   healthy fats ☐ ☐ ☐ ☐
_____   soft drinks ____ coffee____
_____   Sleep # hours _____
Snack: _____   Vitamins Yes ☐   No ☐

Discretionary Calories:
Fast food ☐ ☐ ☐ ☐ ☐   Sweets ☐ ☐ ☐ ☐ ☐
Junk food ☐ ☐ ☐ ☐ ☐   Other ☐ ☐ ☐ ☐ ☐

Thursday water ☐ ☐ ☐ ☐ ☐ ☐ ☐ ☐
Breakfast: _____   dairy ☐ ☐ ☐ ☐ ☐ ☐
_____   veggies ☐ ☐ ☐ ☐ ☐
Lunch: _____   fruit ☐ ☐ ☐ ☐ ☐
_____   protein ☐ ☐ ☐ ☐
Snack: _____   carbs ☐ ☐ ☐ ☐ ☐
Dinner: _____   healthy fats ☐ ☐ ☐ ☐
_____   soft drinks ____ coffee____
_____   Sleep # hours _____
Snack: _____   Vitamins Yes ☐   No ☐

Discretionary Calories:
Fast food ☐ ☐ ☐ ☐ ☐   Sweets ☐ ☐ ☐ ☐ ☐
Junk food ☐ ☐ ☐ ☐ ☐   Other ☐ ☐ ☐ ☐ ☐

Friday water ☐ ☐ ☐ ☐ ☐ ☐ ☐ ☐
Breakfast: _____   dairy ☐ ☐ ☐ ☐ ☐ ☐
_____   veggies ☐ ☐ ☐ ☐
Lunch: _____   fruit ☐ ☐ ☐ ☐ ☐
_____   protein ☐ ☐ ☐ ☐
Snack: _____   carbs ☐ ☐ ☐ ☐ ☐
Dinner: _____   healthy fats ☐ ☐ ☐ ☐
_____   soft drinks ____ coffee____
_____   Sleep # hours _____
Snack: _____   Vitamins Yes ☐   No ☐

Discretionary Calories:
Fast food ☐ ☐ ☐ ☐ ☐   Sweets ☐ ☐ ☐ ☐ ☐
Junk food ☐ ☐ ☐ ☐ ☐   Other ☐ ☐ ☐ ☐ ☐

"Continuous effort is the key to unlocking your potential."
Black Elk, Native American

Saturday water ☐ ☐ ☐ ☐ ☐ ☐ ☐ ☐
Breakfast: _____   dairy ☐ ☐ ☐ ☐ ☐
_____   veggies ☐ ☐ ☐ ☐ ☐
Lunch: _____   fruit ☐ ☐ ☐ ☐ ☐
_____   protein ☐ ☐ ☐ ☐ ☐
Snack: _____   carbs ☐ ☐ ☐ ☐ ☐
Dinner: _____   healthy fats ☐ ☐ ☐ ☐
_____   soft drinks ____ coffee____
_____   Sleep # hours _____
Snack: _____   Vitamins Yes ☐   No ☐

Discretionary Calories:
Fast food ☐ ☐ ☐ ☐ ☐   Sweets ☐ ☐ ☐ ☐ ☐
Junk food ☐ ☐ ☐ ☐ ☐   Other ☐ ☐ ☐ ☐ ☐

Sunday water ☐ ☐ ☐ ☐ ☐ ☐ ☐ ☐
Breakfast: _____   dairy ☐ ☐ ☐ ☐ ☐ ☐
_____   veggies ☐ ☐ ☐ ☐ ☐
Lunch: _____   fruit ☐ ☐ ☐ ☐ ☐
_____   protein ☐ ☐ ☐ ☐ ☐
Snack: _____   carbs ☐ ☐ ☐ ☐ ☐
Dinner: _____   healthy fats ☐ ☐ ☐ ☐
_____   soft drinks ____ coffee____
_____   Sleep # hours _____
Snack: _____   Vitamins Yes ☐   No ☐

Discretionary Calories:
Fast food ☐ ☐ ☐ ☐ ☐   Sweets ☐ ☐ ☐ ☐ ☐
Junk food ☐ ☐ ☐ ☐ ☐   Other ☐ ☐ ☐ ☐ ☐

Try to get in those eight 8 oz. glasses of water everyday!
Start the day with a glass of water, keep a water bottle in your backpack, fill it up at least once throughout the day, drink some water with dinner and finish off the day with a glass of water and you will get in all 8!

Week #2

Name_____

Strength Training Log

Exercises	Date	Date	Exercises	Date	Date
Chest			Arms		
Back			Core		
Shoulders			Legs/Glutes		

Cardio Log

	Cardio	#	Intensity	#
	Exercise	Mins	Level	Miles
Mon				
Tue				
Wed				
Thur				
Fri				
Sat				
Sun				
	Total Minutes	____	Total Miles	____

Nutrition Goal for this week:

_____

Exercise Goal for this week:

_____

© 2009 Betty Kern. Please don't make illegal copies of this page

Other Exercise:

Distance Challenge Miles = _____

Week 3

Monday water ☐☐☐☐☐☐☐☐☐☐
Breakfast: _____
_____ dairy ☐☐☐☐☐
_____ veggies ☐☐☐☐
Lunch: _____ fruit ☐☐☐☐☐
_____ protein ☐☐☐☐
Snack: _____ carbs ☐☐☐☐☐
Dinner: _____ healthy fats ☐☐☐☐
_____ soft drinks ____ coffee ____
_____ Sleep # hours _____
Snack: _____ Vitamins Yes ☐ No ☐
Discretionary Calories:
   Fast food ☐☐☐☐☐   Sweets ☐☐☐☐☐
   Junk food ☐☐☐☐☐   Other ☐☐☐☐☐

Tuesday water ☐☐☐☐☐☐☐☐☐☐
Breakfast: _____ dairy ☐☐☐☐☐
_____ veggies ☐☐☐☐
Lunch: _____ fruit ☐☐☐☐☐
_____ protein ☐☐☐☐
Snack: _____ carbs ☐☐☐☐☐
Dinner: _____ healthy fats ☐☐☐☐
_____ soft drinks ____ coffee ____
_____ Sleep # hours _____
Snack: _____ Vitamins Yes ☐ No ☐
Discretionary Calories:
   Fast food ☐☐☐☐☐   Sweets ☐☐☐☐☐
   Junk food ☐☐☐☐☐   Other ☐☐☐☐☐

In the middle of the afternoon when you feel tired, resist the temptation to grab a coffee, candy bar or a soft drink…try one of these for an energy boost!
- Take a walk
- Take several deep breaths
- Do as many push-ups as you can
- Do a few dozen sit-ups or crunches
- Have a healthy low-fat snack rich in protein & carbohydrates…yogurt with fruit, apple slices w/peanut butter, carrot slices w/ hummus, nuts & raisins

Wednesday water ☐☐☐☐☐☐☐☐☐☐
Breakfast: _____ dairy ☐☐☐☐☐
_____ veggies ☐☐☐☐
Lunch: _____ fruit ☐☐☐☐☐
_____ protein ☐☐☐☐
Snack: _____ carbs ☐☐☐☐☐
Dinner: _____ healthy fats ☐☐☐☐
_____ soft drinks ____ coffee ____
_____ Sleep # hours _____
Snack: _____ Vitamins Yes ☐ No ☐
Discretionary Calories:
   Fast food ☐☐☐☐☐   Sweets ☐☐☐☐☐
   Junk food ☐☐☐☐☐   Other ☐☐☐☐☐

Thursday water ☐☐☐☐☐☐☐☐☐☐
Breakfast: _____ dairy ☐☐☐☐☐
_____ veggies ☐☐☐☐
Lunch: _____ fruit ☐☐☐☐☐
_____ protein ☐☐☐☐
Snack: _____ carbs ☐☐☐☐☐
Dinner: _____ healthy fats ☐☐☐☐
_____ soft drinks ____ coffee ____
_____ Sleep # hours _____
Snack: _____ Vitamins Yes ☐ No ☐
Discretionary Calories:
   Fast food ☐☐☐☐☐   Sweets ☐☐☐☐☐
   Junk food ☐☐☐☐☐   Other ☐☐☐☐☐

Friday water ☐☐☐☐☐☐☐☐☐☐
Breakfast: _____ dairy ☐☐☐☐☐
_____ veggies ☐☐☐☐
Lunch: _____ fruit ☐☐☐☐☐
_____ protein ☐☐☐☐
Snack: _____ carbs ☐☐☐☐☐
Dinner: _____ healthy fats ☐☐☐☐
_____ soft drinks ____ coffee ____
_____ Sleep # hours _____
Snack: _____ Vitamins Yes ☐ No ☐
Discretionary Calories:
   Fast food ☐☐☐☐☐   Sweets ☐☐☐☐☐
   Junk food ☐☐☐☐☐   Other ☐☐☐☐☐

"The first wealth is health."
Ralph Waldo Emerson
Everyday take the opportunity to make an investment in your health/wealth…you are worth it!

Saturday water ☐☐☐☐☐☐☐☐☐☐
Breakfast: _____ dairy ☐☐☐☐☐
_____ veggies ☐☐☐☐
Lunch: _____ fruit ☐☐☐☐☐
_____ protein ☐☐☐☐
Snack: _____ carbs ☐☐☐☐☐
Dinner: _____ healthy fats ☐☐☐☐
_____ soft drinks ____ coffee ____
_____ Sleep # hours _____
Snack: _____ Vitamins Yes ☐ No ☐
Discretionary Calories:
   Fast food ☐☐☐☐☐   Sweets ☐☐☐☐☐
   Junk food ☐☐☐☐☐   Other ☐☐☐☐☐

Sunday water ☐☐☐☐☐☐☐☐☐☐
Breakfast: _____ dairy ☐☐☐☐☐
_____ veggies ☐☐☐☐
Lunch: _____ fruit ☐☐☐☐☐
_____ protein ☐☐☐☐
Snack: _____ carbs ☐☐☐☐☐
Dinner: _____ healthy fats ☐☐☐☐
_____ soft drinks ____ coffee ____
_____ Sleep # hours _____
Snack: _____ Vitamins Yes ☐ No ☐
Discretionary Calories:
   Fast food ☐☐☐☐☐   Sweets ☐☐☐☐☐
   Junk food ☐☐☐☐☐   Other ☐☐☐☐☐

How are your workouts going?

Are you getting in some exercise on the weekend?

Find a friend or family member to workout with…it will be more fun and he/she will help you make it a habit!

Week #3　　　　　　　　　　Name_____

Strength Training Log

Exercises	Date	Date	Exercises	Date	Date
Chest			Arms		
Back			Core		
Shoulders			Legs/Glutes		

Cardio Log

	Cardio Exercise	# Mins	Intensity Level	# Miles
Mon				
Tue				
Wed				
Thur				
Fri				
Sat				
Sun				
	Total Minutes	_____	Total Miles	_____

Nutrition Goal for this week:

_____

Exercise Goal for this week:

_____

© 2009 Betty Kern. Please don't make illegal copies of this page

Other Exercise:

Distance Challenge Miles = _____

Week 4

Monday water ☐☐☐☐☐☐☐☐☐
Breakfast: _____ dairy ☐☐☐☐☐☐
_____ veggies ☐☐☐☐☐☐
Lunch: _____ fruit ☐☐☐☐☐
_____ protein ☐☐☐☐
Snack: _____ carbs ☐☐☐☐☐☐
Dinner: _____ healthy fats ☐☐☐☐☐
_____ soft drinks ___ coffee __
_____ Sleep # hours _____
Snack: _____ Vitamins Yes ☐ No ☐
Discretionary Calories:
   Fast food ☐☐☐☐☐   Sweets ☐☐☐☐☐
   Junk food ☐☐☐☐☐   Other ☐☐☐☐☐

Tuesday water ☐☐☐☐☐☐☐☐☐
Breakfast: _____ dairy ☐☐☐☐☐☐
_____ veggies ☐☐☐☐☐☐
Lunch: _____ fruit ☐☐☐☐☐
_____ protein ☐☐☐☐
Snack: _____ carbs ☐☐☐☐☐☐
Dinner: _____ healthy fats ☐☐☐☐☐
_____ soft drinks __ coffee __
_____ Sleep # hours _____
Snack: _____ Vitamins Yes ☐ No
Discretionary Calories:
   Fast food ☐☐☐☐☐   Sweets ☐☐☐☐☐
   Junk food ☐☐☐☐☐   Other ☐☐☐☐☐

Are you getting enough sleep?

Lack of sleep is a contributing cause to becoming overweight or obese. When you do not get enough sleep, your body produces less of the hormone that restricts appetite and more of the hormone that stimulates appetite! Guess what that leads to…over eating and weight gain! Get plenty of shut-eye!

Wednesday water ☐☐☐☐☐☐☐☐☐
Breakfast: _____ dairy ☐☐☐☐☐
_____ veggies ☐☐☐☐
Lunch: _____ fruit ☐☐☐☐☐
_____ protein ☐☐☐☐
Snack: _____ carbs ☐☐☐☐☐☐
Dinner: _____ healthy fats ☐☐☐☐
_____ soft drinks ___ coffee __
_____ Sleep # hours _____
Snack: _____ Vitamins Yes ☐ No ☐
Discretionary Calories:
   Fast food ☐☐☐☐☐   Sweets ☐☐☐☐☐
   Junk food ☐☐☐☐☐   Other ☐☐☐☐☐

Thursday water ☐☐☐☐☐☐☐☐☐
Breakfast: _____ dairy ☐☐☐☐☐
_____ veggies ☐☐☐☐
Lunch: _____ fruit ☐☐☐☐☐
_____ protein ☐☐☐☐
Snack: _____ carbs ☐☐☐☐☐☐
Dinner: _____ healthy fats ☐☐☐☐
_____ soft drinks ___ coffee __
_____ Sleep # hours _____
Snack: _____ Vitamins Yes ☐ No ☐
Discretionary Calories:
   Fast food ☐☐☐☐☐   Sweets ☐☐☐☐☐
   Junk food ☐☐☐☐☐   Other ☐☐☐☐☐

Friday water ☐☐☐☐☐☐☐☐☐
Breakfast: _____ dairy ☐☐☐☐☐
_____ veggies ☐☐☐☐
Lunch: _____ fruit ☐☐☐☐☐
_____ protein ☐☐☐☐
Snack: _____ carbs ☐☐☐☐☐☐
Dinner: _____ healthy fats ☐☐☐☐
_____ soft drinks ___ coffee __
_____ Sleep # hours _____
Snack: _____ Vitamins Yes ☐ No ☐
Discretionary Calories:
   Fast food ☐☐☐☐☐   Sweets ☐☐☐☐☐
   Junk food ☐☐☐☐☐   Other ☐☐☐☐☐

Motivation is what gets you started…
Habit is what keeps you going!

Saturday water ☐☐☐☐☐☐☐☐☐
Breakfast: _____ dairy ☐☐☐☐
_____ veggies ☐☐☐☐
Lunch: _____ fruit ☐☐☐☐☐
_____ protein ☐☐☐☐
Snack: _____ carbs ☐☐☐☐☐
Dinner: _____ healthy fats ☐☐☐☐
_____ soft drinks ___ coffee __
_____ Sleep # hours _____
Snack: _____ Vitamins Yes ☐ No ☐
Discretionary Calories:
   Fast food ☐☐☐☐☐   Sweets ☐☐☐☐☐
   Junk food ☐☐☐☐☐   Other ☐☐☐☐☐

Sunday water ☐☐☐☐☐☐☐☐☐
Breakfast: _____ dairy ☐☐☐☐☐
_____ veggies ☐☐☐☐
Lunch: _____ fruit ☐☐☐☐☐
_____ protein ☐☐☐☐
Snack: _____ carbs ☐☐☐☐☐
Dinner: _____ healthy fats ☐☐☐☐
_____ soft drinks ___ coffee __
_____ Sleep # hours _____
Snack: _____ Vitamins Yes ☐ No ☐
Discretionary Calories:
   Fast food ☐☐☐☐☐   Sweets ☐☐☐☐☐
   Junk food ☐☐☐☐☐   Other ☐☐☐☐☐

Distance Challenge Miles = _____

What is one thing you are doing different with your nutritional habits since starting this class?

Week #4

Name_____

Strength Training Log

Exercises	Date	Date	Exercises	Date	Date
Chest			Arms		
Back			Core		
Shoulders			Legs/Glutes		

Other Exercise:

Cardio Log

	Cardio Exercise	# Mins	Intensity Level	# Miles
Mon				
Tue				
Wed				
Thur				
Fri				
Sat				
Sun				
	Total Minutes	____	Total Miles	____

Nutrition Goal for this week:

_____

Exercise Goal for this week:

_____

© 2009 Betty Kern. Please don't make illegal copies of this page

Distance Challenge Miles = _____

My Pyramid Tracker Assignment

Return to the web site www.MyPyramid.gov.
Go to the section **My Pyramid Tracker**.
Enter in 24 hours worth of physical activity and eating habits.

1. Click on **"Assess Your Food Intake."**
    Enter the foods you have eaten in a 24-hour period including the amount you ate.
    Analyze the intake under **"My Pyramid Recommendations"** and **print** out the results.
    Next click on the **"Nutrient Intake"** at the bottom of the page and **print** out the results.

2. Go to the **"Physical Activity"** section and click on **"Standard Option."**
    Calculate your physical activity score by entering in any physical activity for the last 24 hours.
    Click on **"Physical Activity Analysis"** and determine your physical activity score.
    Print out the page with your **"Physical Activity Score."**

3. At the top of the Physical Activity page, select **"Energy Balance Analysis."**
    Calculate your **"Energy Balance"** and **print** out the results.

    *You should have **four** pages to turn in for this assignment.*
    Make sure your name is on all four pages and staple them together.

4. On the back of the last page, answer the following:
    How are you doing with your nutrition and exercise habits?
    Are you meeting the pyramid recommendations?
    In what areas of nutrition are you doing well?
    What areas of your diet do you need to improve? (give specifics)
    Are you meeting the recommendations for physical activity?
    How could you improve your physical activity habits?

89

Week 5

Monday water ☐☐☐☐☐☐☐☐☐☐
Breakfast: _____ dairy ☐☐☐☐☐
_____ veggies ☐☐☐☐☐
Lunch: _____ fruit ☐☐☐☐☐
_____ protein ☐☐☐☐
Snack: _____ carbs ☐☐☐☐☐
Dinner: _____ healthy fats ☐☐☐☐
_____ soft drinks __ coffee __
_____ Sleep # hours _____
Snack: _____ Vitamins Yes ☐ No ☐
Discretionary Calories:
   Fast food ☐☐☐☐☐   Sweets ☐☐☐☐☐
   Junk food ☐☐☐☐☐   Other ☐☐☐☐☐

Tuesday water ☐☐☐☐☐☐☐☐☐☐
Breakfast: _____ dairy ☐☐☐☐☐
_____ veggies ☐☐☐☐☐
Lunch: _____ fruit ☐☐☐☐☐
_____ protein ☐☐☐☐
Snack: _____ carbs ☐☐☐☐☐
Dinner: _____ healthy fats ☐☐☐☐
_____ soft drinks __ coffee __
_____ Sleep # hours _____
Snack: _____ Vitamins Yes ☐ No ☐
Discretionary Calories:
   Fast food ☐☐☐☐☐   Sweets ☐☐☐☐☐
   Junk food ☐☐☐☐☐   Other ☐☐☐☐☐

Remember energy balance is the goal!

In other words…
…if you want to maintain your current weight, energy in must equal energy out (caloric balance)
…if you want to lose weight, energy in must be less than energy out (negative caloric balance)
…if you want to gain weight, energy in must be greater than energy out (positive caloric balance)

Wednesday water ☐☐☐☐☐☐☐☐☐☐
Breakfast: _____ dairy ☐☐☐☐☐
_____ veggies ☐☐☐☐☐
Lunch: _____ fruit ☐☐☐☐☐
_____ protein ☐☐☐☐
Snack: _____ carbs ☐☐☐☐☐
Dinner: _____ healthy fats ☐☐☐☐
_____ soft drinks __ coffee __
_____ Sleep # hours _____
Snack: _____ Vitamins Yes ☐ No ☐
Discretionary Calories:
   Fast food ☐☐☐☐☐   Sweets ☐☐☐☐☐
   Junk food ☐☐☐☐☐   Other ☐☐☐☐☐

Thursday water ☐☐☐☐☐☐☐☐☐☐
Breakfast: _____ dairy ☐☐☐☐☐
_____ veggies ☐☐☐☐☐
Lunch: _____ fruit ☐☐☐☐☐
_____ protein ☐☐☐☐
Snack: _____ carbs ☐☐☐☐☐
Dinner: _____ healthy fats ☐☐☐☐
_____ soft drinks __ coffee __
_____ Sleep # hours _____
Snack: _____ Vitamins Yes ☐ No ☐
Discretionary Calories:
   Fast food ☐☐☐☐☐   Sweets ☐☐☐☐☐
   Junk food ☐☐☐☐☐   Other ☐☐☐☐☐

Friday water ☐☐☐☐☐☐☐☐☐☐
Breakfast: _____ dairy ☐☐☐☐☐
_____ veggies ☐☐☐☐☐
Lunch: _____ fruit ☐☐☐☐☐
_____ protein ☐☐☐☐
Snack: _____ carbs ☐☐☐☐☐
Dinner: _____ healthy fats ☐☐☐☐
_____ soft drinks __ coffee __
_____ Sleep # hours _____
Snack: _____ Vitamins Yes ☐ No ☐
Discretionary Calories:
   Fast food ☐☐☐☐☐   Sweets ☐☐☐☐☐
   Junk food ☐☐☐☐☐   Other ☐☐☐☐☐

"Life is like riding a bicycle. To keep your balance you must keep moving."
Albert Einstein

Saturday water ☐☐☐☐☐☐☐☐☐☐
Breakfast: _____ dairy ☐☐☐☐☐
_____ veggies ☐☐☐☐☐
Lunch: _____ fruit ☐☐☐☐☐
_____ protein ☐☐☐☐
Snack: _____ carbs ☐☐☐☐☐
Dinner: _____ healthy fats ☐☐☐☐
_____ soft drinks __ coffee __
_____ Sleep # hours _____
Snack: _____ Vitamins Yes ☐ No ☐
Discretionary Calories:
   Fast food ☐☐☐☐☐   Sweets ☐☐☐☐☐
   Junk food ☐☐☐☐☐   Other ☐☐☐☐☐

Sunday water ☐☐☐☐☐☐☐☐☐☐
Breakfast: _____ dairy ☐☐☐☐☐
_____ veggies ☐☐☐☐☐
Lunch: _____ fruit ☐☐☐☐☐
_____ protein ☐☐☐☐
Snack: _____ carbs ☐☐☐☐☐
Dinner: _____ healthy fats ☐☐☐☐
_____ soft drinks __ coffee __
_____ Sleep # hours _____
Snack: _____ Vitamins Yes ☐ No ☐
Discretionary Calories:
   Fast food ☐☐☐☐☐   Sweets ☐☐☐☐☐
   Junk food ☐☐☐☐☐   Other ☐☐☐☐☐

How is the good nutrition going?
About the same ☐ Good ☐ Better ☐ Bad ☐

Try to get all of the servings of the different food groups daily. As we will discuss, good nutrition along with exercise can help you not only look and feel better but will also help you remain disease free!

Week #5

Name_____

Strength Training Log

Exercises	Date	Date	Exercises	Date	Date
Chest			Arms		
Back			Core		
Shoulders			Legs/Glutes		

Cardio Log

	Cardio	#	Intensity	#
	Exercise	Mins	Level	Miles
Mon				
Tue				
Wed				
Thur				
Fri				
Sat				
Sun				
	Total		Total	
	Minutes	____	Miles	____

Nutrition Goal for this week:

_____

Exercise Goal for this week:

_____

© 2009 Betty Kern. Please don't make illegal copies of this page

Other Exercise:

Distance Challenge Miles = _____

Week 6

Monday water ☐☐☐☐☐☐☐☐
Breakfast: _____ dairy ☐☐☐☐☐
_____ veggies ☐☐☐☐☐
Lunch: _____ fruit ☐☐☐☐☐
_____ protein ☐☐☐☐
Snack: _____ carbs ☐☐☐☐☐
Dinner: _____ healthy fats ☐☐☐☐
_____ soft drinks __ coffee__
_____ Sleep # hours _____
Snack: _____ Vitamins Yes ☐ No ☐

Discretionary Calories:
   Fast food ☐☐☐☐☐   Sweets ☐☐☐☐☐
   Junk food ☐☐☐☐☐   Other ☐☐☐☐☐

Tuesday water ☐☐☐☐☐☐☐☐☐
Breakfast: _____ dairy ☐☐☐☐☐
_____ veggies ☐☐☐☐☐
Lunch: _____ fruit ☐☐☐☐☐
_____ protein ☐☐☐☐
Snack: _____ carbs ☐☐☐☐☐
Dinner: _____ healthy fats ☐☐☐☐
_____ soft drinks __ coffee_
_____ Sleep # hours _____
Snack: _____ Vitamins Yes ☐ No ☐

Discretionary Calories:
   Fast food ☐☐☐☐☐   Sweets ☐☐☐☐☐
   Junk food ☐☐☐☐☐   Other ☐☐☐☐☐

Are you noticing any changes in your body?

Are you noticing any changes in the quality of your sleep?

Are you noticing any changes in your energy level?

Are you noticing any changes in your attitude?

Wednesday water ☐☐☐☐☐☐☐☐☐
Breakfast: _____ dairy ☐☐☐☐☐
_____ veggies ☐☐☐☐☐
Lunch: _____ fruit ☐☐☐☐☐
_____ protein ☐☐☐☐
Snack: _____ carbs ☐☐☐☐☐
Dinner: _____ healthy fats ☐☐☐☐
_____ soft drinks __ coffee__
_____ Sleep # hours _____
Snack: _____ Vitamins Yes ☐ No ☐

Discretionary Calories:
   Fast food ☐☐☐☐☐   Sweets ☐☐☐☐☐
   Junk food ☐☐☐☐☐   Other ☐☐☐☐☐

Thursday water ☐☐☐☐☐☐☐☐☐
Breakfast: _____ dairy ☐☐☐☐☐
_____ veggies ☐☐☐☐☐
Lunch: _____ fruit ☐☐☐☐☐
_____ protein ☐☐☐☐
Snack: _____ carbs ☐☐☐☐☐
Dinner: _____ healthy fats ☐☐☐☐
_____ soft drinks __ coffee__
_____ Sleep # hours _____
Snack: _____ Vitamins Yes ☐ No ☐

Discretionary Calories:
   Fast food ☐☐☐☐☐   Sweets ☐☐☐☐☐
   Junk food ☐☐☐☐☐   Other ☐☐☐☐☐

Friday water ☐☐☐☐☐☐☐☐☐
Breakfast: _____ dairy ☐☐☐☐☐
_____ veggies ☐☐☐☐☐
Lunch: _____ fruit ☐☐☐☐☐
_____ protein ☐☐☐☐
Snack: _____ carbs ☐☐☐☐☐
Dinner: _____ healthy fats ☐☐☐☐
_____ soft drinks __ coffee__
_____ Sleep # hours _____
Snack: _____ Vitamins Yes ☐ No ☐

Discretionary Calories:
   Fast food ☐☐☐☐☐   Sweets ☐☐☐☐☐
   Junk food ☐☐☐☐☐   Other ☐☐☐☐☐

"Eating right isn't about willpower; it is about changing bad habits."
Denise Austin

Saturday water ☐☐☐☐☐☐☐☐☐
Breakfast: _____ dairy ☐☐☐☐☐
_____ veggies ☐☐☐☐☐
Lunch: _____ fruit ☐☐☐☐☐
_____ protein ☐☐☐☐
Snack: _____ carbs ☐☐☐☐☐
Dinner: _____ healthy fats ☐☐☐☐
_____ soft drinks __ coffee__
_____ Sleep # hours ___
Snack: _____ Vitamins Yes ☐ No ☐

Discretionary Calories:
   Fast food ☐☐☐☐☐   Sweets ☐☐☐☐☐
   Junk food ☐☐☐☐☐   Other ☐☐☐☐☐

Sunday water ☐☐☐☐☐☐☐☐☐
Breakfast: _____ dairy ☐☐☐☐☐
_____ veggies ☐☐☐☐☐
Lunch: _____ fruit ☐☐☐☐☐
_____ protein ☐☐☐☐
Snack: _____ carbs ☐☐☐☐☐
Dinner: _____ healthy fats ☐☐☐☐
_____ soft drinks __ coffee__
_____ Sleep # hours _____
Snack: _____ Vitamins Yes ☐ No ☐

Discretionary Calories:
   Fast food ☐☐☐☐☐   Sweets ☐☐☐☐☐
   Junk food ☐☐☐☐☐   Other ☐☐☐☐☐

Are you noticing any changes in your school work or grades?

Has your family noticed any improvement in these areas?

Distance Challenge Miles = _____

Week #6

Name_____

Strength Training Log

Exercises	Date	Date	Exercises	Date	Date
Chest			Arms		
Back			Core		
Shoulders			Legs/Glutes		

Cardio Log

	Cardio	#	Intensity	#
	Exercise	Mins	Level	Miles
Mon				
Tue				
Wed				
Thur				
Fri				
Sat				
Sun				
	Total Minutes	____	Total Miles	____

Nutrition Goal for this week:

_____

Exercise Goal for this week:

_____

© 2009 Betty Kern. Please don't make illegal copies of this page

Other Exercise:

Distance Challenge Miles = _____

Week 7

Monday water ☐☐☐☐☐☐☐☐☐
Breakfast: _____ dairy ☐☐☐☐☐
_____ veggies ☐☐☐☐☐
Lunch: _____ fruit ☐☐☐☐☐
_____ protein ☐☐☐☐☐
Snack: _____ carbs ☐☐☐☐☐
Dinner: _____ healthy fats ☐☐☐☐
_____ soft drinks __ coffee __
_____ Sleep # hours _____
Snack: _____ Vitamins Yes ☐   No ☐

Discretionary Calories:
Fast food ☐☐☐☐   Sweets ☐☐☐☐☐
Junk food ☐☐☐☐☐   Other ☐☐☐☐☐

Tuesday water ☐☐☐☐☐☐☐☐☐
Breakfast: _____ dairy ☐☐☐☐☐
_____ veggies ☐☐☐☐☐
Lunch: _____ fruit ☐☐☐☐☐
_____ protein ☐☐☐☐
Snack: _____ carbs ☐☐☐☐☐
Dinner: _____ healthy fats ☐☐☐☐
_____ soft drinks __ coffee __
_____ Sleep # hours _____
Snack: _____ Vitamins Yes ☐ No ☐

Discretionary Calories:
Fast food ☐☐☐☐   Sweets ☐☐☐☐☐
Junk food ☐☐☐☐☐   Other ☐☐☐☐☐

Habits to Help Shrink Your Middle
(Prevention 2007)

1. Calm down. Stress contributes to fat storage around your belly!
2. Don't smoke. Smokers have more abdominal fat than nonsmokers.
3. Eat more fiber…24-35g per day…eat whole grains, fruits and vegetables.
4. Drink more water! Soft drinks will bloat your belly!
5. Keep bones strong…with calcium & exercise
6. Get your heart rate up…aerobic exercise is needed to reduce fat storage…45 – 60 minutes five times a week! →

Wednesday water ☐☐☐☐☐☐☐☐☐
Breakfast: _____ dairy ☐☐☐☐☐
_____ veggies ☐☐☐☐☐
Lunch: _____ fruit ☐☐☐☐☐
_____ protein ☐☐☐☐☐
Snack: _____ carbs ☐☐☐☐☐
Dinner: _____ healthy fats ☐☐☐☐
_____ soft drinks __ coffee __
_____ Sleep # hours _____
Snack: _____ Vitamins Yes ☐   No ☐

Discretionary Calories:
Fast food ☐☐☐☐☐   Sweets ☐☐☐☐☐
Junk food ☐☐☐☐☐   Other ☐☐☐☐☐

Thursday water ☐☐☐☐☐☐☐☐☐
Breakfast: _____ dairy ☐☐☐☐☐
_____ veggies ☐☐☐☐☐
Lunch: _____ fruit ☐☐☐☐☐
_____ protein ☐☐☐☐☐
Snack: _____ carbs ☐☐☐☐☐
Dinner: _____ healthy fats ☐☐☐☐
_____ soft drinks __ coffee __
_____ Sleep # hours _____
Snack: _____ Vitamins Yes ☐   No ☐

Discretionary Calories:
Fast food ☐☐☐☐☐   Sweets ☐☐☐☐☐
Junk food ☐☐☐☐☐   Other ☐☐☐☐☐

Friday water ☐☐☐☐☐☐☐☐☐
Breakfast: _____ dairy ☐☐☐☐☐
_____ veggies ☐☐☐☐☐
Lunch: _____ fruit ☐☐☐☐☐
_____ protein ☐☐☐☐☐
Snack: _____ carbs ☐☐☐☐☐
Dinner: _____ healthy fats ☐☐☐☐
_____ soft drinks __ coffee __
_____ Sleep # hours _____
Snack: _____ Vitamins Yes ☐   No ☐

Discretionary Calories:
Fast food ☐☐☐☐☐   Sweets ☐☐☐☐☐
Junk food ☐☐☐☐☐   Other ☐☐☐☐☐

"Exercise boosts fat burning because your muscles become trained over time to use more fat as fuel." Liz Applegate RD

Saturday water ☐☐☐☐☐☐☐☐☐
Breakfast: _____ dairy ☐☐☐☐☐
_____ veggies ☐☐☐☐☐
Lunch: _____ fruit ☐☐☐☐☐
_____ protein ☐☐☐☐☐
Snack: _____ carbs ☐☐☐☐☐
Dinner: _____ healthy fats ☐☐☐☐
_____ soft drinks __ coffee __
_____ Sleep # hours _____
Snack: _____ Vitamins Yes ☐   No ☐

Discretionary Calories:
Fast food ☐☐☐☐☐   Sweets ☐☐☐☐☐
Junk food ☐☐☐☐☐   Other ☐☐☐☐☐

Sunday water ☐☐☐☐☐☐☐☐☐
Breakfast: _____ dairy ☐☐☐☐☐
_____ veggies ☐☐☐☐☐
Lunch: _____ fruit ☐☐☐☐☐
_____ protein ☐☐☐☐☐
Snack: _____ carbs ☐☐☐☐☐
Dinner: _____ healthy fats ☐☐☐☐
_____ soft drinks __ coffee __
_____ Sleep # hours _____
Snack: _____ Vitamins Yes ☐   No ☐

Discretionary Calories:
Fast food ☐☐☐☐☐   Sweets ☐☐☐☐☐
Junk food ☐☐☐☐☐   Other ☐☐☐☐☐

7. Tuck that tummy…stand or sit up tall and pull your belly button towards your spine!
8. Hit the weights…weight training will continue to burn fat stores and sculpt muscle.
9. Add in an extra ab workout! Once or twice each week add in a 20-minute ab workout! The results will be amazing!
10. Mix up your workouts…include yoga, Pilates, kick boxing, ball workouts…it will constantly challenge your ab muscles and produce results!

Week #7

Name_____

Strength Training Log

Exercises	Date	Date	Exercises	Date	Date
Chest			Arms		
Back			Core		
Shoulders			Legs/Glutes		

Cardio Log

	Cardio	#	Intensity	#
	Exercise	Mins	Level	Miles
Mon				
Tue				
Wed				
Thur				
Fri				
Sat				
Sun				
	Total Minutes	____	Total Miles	____

Nutrition Goal for this week:

_____

Exercise Goal for this week:

_____

© 2009 Betty Kern. Please don't make illegal copies of this page

Other Exercise:

Distance Challenge Miles = _____

Week 8

Monday water ☐☐☐☐☐☐☐☐☐☐
- Breakfast: _____ dairy ☐☐☐☐☐
- _____ veggies ☐☐☐☐☐
- Lunch: _____ fruit ☐☐☐☐☐
- _____ protein ☐☐☐☐
- Snack: _____ carbs ☐☐☐☐☐
- Dinner: _____ healthy fats ☐☐☐☐
- _____ soft drinks __ coffee __
- _____ Sleep # hours _____
- Snack: _____ Vitamins Yes ☐ No ☐
- Discretionary Calories:
  - Fast food ☐☐☐☐☐   Sweets ☐☐☐☐☐
  - Junk food ☐☐☐☐☐   Other ☐☐☐☐☐

Tuesday water ☐☐☐☐☐☐☐☐☐☐
- Breakfast: _____ dairy ☐☐☐☐☐
- _____ veggies ☐☐☐☐☐
- Lunch: _____ fruit ☐☐☐☐☐
- _____ protein ☐☐☐☐
- Snack: _____ carbs ☐☐☐☐☐
- Dinner: _____ healthy fats ☐☐☐☐
- _____ soft drinks __ coffee __
- _____ Sleep # hours _____
- Snack: _____ Vitamins Yes ☐ No ☐
- Discretionary Calories:
  - Fast food ☐☐☐☐☐   Sweets ☐☐☐☐☐
  - Junk food ☐☐☐☐☐   Other ☐☐☐☐☐

Distance Challenge Mile Total = _____

Are you enjoying the challenge?

What are you doing to get in extra miles?

Who is walking or running with you?

Wednesday water ☐☐☐☐☐☐☐☐☐☐
- Breakfast: _____ dairy ☐☐☐☐☐
- _____ veggies ☐☐☐☐
- Lunch: _____ fruit ☐☐☐☐☐
- _____ protein ☐☐☐☐
- Snack: _____ carbs ☐☐☐☐☐
- Dinner: _____ healthy fats ☐☐☐☐
- _____ soft drinks __ coffee __
- _____ Sleep # hours _____
- Snack: _____ Vitamins Yes ☐ No ☐
- Discretionary Calories:
  - Fast food ☐☐☐☐☐   Sweets ☐☐☐☐☐
  - Junk food ☐☐☐☐☐   Other ☐☐☐☐☐

Thursday water ☐☐☐☐☐☐☐☐☐☐
- Breakfast: _____ dairy ☐☐☐☐☐
- _____ veggies ☐☐☐☐
- Lunch: _____ fruit ☐☐☐☐☐
- _____ protein ☐☐☐☐
- Snack: _____ carbs ☐☐☐☐☐
- Dinner: _____ healthy fats ☐☐☐☐
- _____ soft drinks __ coffee __
- _____ Sleep # hours _____
- Snack: _____ Vitamins Yes ☐ No ☐
- Discretionary Calories:
  - Fast food ☐☐☐☐☐   Sweets ☐☐☐☐☐
  - Junk food ☐☐☐☐☐   Other ☐☐☐☐☐

Friday water ☐☐☐☐☐☐☐☐☐☐
- Breakfast: _____ dairy ☐☐☐☐☐
- _____ veggies ☐☐☐☐
- Lunch: _____ fruit ☐☐☐☐☐
- _____ protein ☐☐☐☐
- Snack: _____ carbs ☐☐☐☐☐
- Dinner: _____ healthy fats ☐☐☐☐
- _____ soft drinks __ coffee __
- _____ Sleep # hours _____
- Snack: _____ Vitamins Yes ☐ No ☐
- Discretionary Calories:
  - Fast food ☐☐☐☐☐   Sweets ☐☐☐☐☐
  - Junk food ☐☐☐☐☐   Other ☐☐☐☐☐

"Something is better than nothing...even if you can only do a short workout...do something!"
Betty Kern, MS, CSCS

Saturday water ☐☐☐☐☐☐☐☐☐☐
- Breakfast: _____ dairy ☐☐☐☐☐
- _____ veggies ☐☐☐☐
- Lunch: _____ fruit ☐☐☐☐☐
- _____ protein ☐☐☐☐
- Snack: _____ carbs ☐☐☐☐☐
- Dinner: _____ healthy fats ☐☐☐☐
- _____ soft drinks __ coffee __
- _____ Sleep # hours _____
- Snack: _____ Vitamins Yes ☐ No ☐
- Discretionary Calories:
  - Fast food ☐☐☐☐☐   Sweets ☐☐☐☐☐
  - Junk food ☐☐☐☐☐   Other ☐☐☐☐☐

Sunday water ☐☐☐☐☐☐☐☐☐☐
- Breakfast: _____ dairy ☐☐☐☐☐
- _____ veggies ☐☐☐☐
- Lunch: _____ fruit ☐☐☐☐☐
- _____ protein ☐☐☐☐
- Snack: _____ carbs ☐☐☐☐☐
- Dinner: _____ healthy fats ☐☐☐☐
- _____ soft drinks __ coffee __
- _____ Sleep # hours _____
- Snack: _____ Vitamins Yes ☐ No ☐
- Discretionary Calories:
  - Fast food ☐☐☐☐☐   Sweets ☐☐☐☐☐
  - Junk food ☐☐☐☐☐   Other ☐☐☐☐☐

What is your favorite activity that we have done in class?

Are there any new activities or type exercise you would like us to do in class?

Week #8

Name_____

Strength Training Log

Exercises	Date	Date	Exercises	Date	Date
Chest			Arms		
Back			Core		
Shoulders			Legs/Glutes		

Other Exercise:

Cardio Log

	Cardio Exercise	# Mins	Intensity Level	# Miles
Mon				
Tue				
Wed				
Thur				
Fri				
Sat				
Sun				
	Total Minutes ____		Total Miles ____	

Nutrition Goal for this week:

_____

Exercise Goal for this week:

_____

© 2009 Betty Kern. Please don't make illegal copies of this page

Distance Challenge Miles = _____

Week 9

Monday water ☐☐☐☐☐☐☐☐
Breakfast: _____ dairy ☐☐☐☐☐
_____ veggies ☐☐☐☐☐
Lunch: _____ fruit ☐☐☐☐
_____ protein ☐☐☐☐
Snack: _____ carbs ☐☐☐☐☐
Dinner: _____ healthy fats ☐☐☐☐
_____ soft drinks___ coffee___
_____ Sleep # hours _____
Snack: _____ Vitamins Yes ☐ No ☐
Discretionary Calories:
  Fast food ☐☐☐☐☐   Sweets ☐☐☐☐☐
  Junk food ☐☐☐☐☐   Other ☐☐☐☐☐

Tuesday water ☐☐☐☐☐☐☐☐
Breakfast: _____ dairy ☐☐☐☐☐
_____ veggies ☐☐☐☐☐
Lunch: _____ fruit ☐☐☐☐
_____ protein ☐☐☐☐
Snack: _____ carbs ☐☐☐☐☐
Dinner: _____ healthy fats ☐☐☐☐
_____ soft drinks___ coffee_
_____ Sleep # hours _____
Snack: _____ Vitamins Yes ☐ No ☐
Discretionary Calories:
  Fast food ☐☐☐☐☐   Sweets ☐☐☐☐☐
  Junk food ☐☐☐☐☐   Other ☐☐☐☐☐

Sneaky ways to burn more calories each day!
1. Fidget! A lot! Studies have shown that people who fidget can burn up to 350 more calories a day!
2. Stand up while talking on the phone!
3. Take the stairs…everywhere!
4. Park farther away from the doors in a parking lot.
5. Get up and walk around at least five times a day for 10 minutes.
6. Add in some new habits…do 25 lunges, squats and crunches along with 10 push-ups before you get in the shower or go to bed!

Wednesday water ☐☐☐☐☐☐☐☐
Breakfast: _____ dairy ☐☐☐☐☐
_____ veggies ☐☐☐☐☐
Lunch: _____ fruit ☐☐☐☐
_____ protein ☐☐☐☐
Snack: _____ carbs ☐☐☐☐☐
Dinner: _____ healthy fats ☐☐☐☐
_____ soft drinks ___ coffee___
_____ Sleep # hours _____
Snack: _____ Vitamins Yes ☐ No ☐
Discretionary Calories:
  Fast food ☐☐☐☐☐   Sweets ☐☐☐☐☐
  Junk food ☐☐☐☐☐   Other ☐☐☐☐☐

Thursday water ☐☐☐☐☐☐☐☐
Breakfast: _____ dairy ☐☐☐☐☐
_____ veggies ☐☐☐☐☐
Lunch: _____ fruit ☐☐☐☐
_____ protein ☐☐☐☐
Snack: _____ carbs ☐☐☐☐☐
Dinner: _____ healthy fats ☐☐☐☐
_____ soft drinks ___ coffee___
_____ Sleep # hours _____
Snack: _____ Vitamins Yes ☐ No ☐
Discretionary Calories:
  Fast food ☐☐☐☐☐   Sweets ☐☐☐☐☐
  Junk food ☐☐☐☐☐   Other ☐☐☐☐☐

Friday water ☐☐☐☐☐☐☐☐
Breakfast: _____ dairy ☐☐☐☐☐
_____ veggies ☐☐☐☐
Lunch: _____ fruit ☐☐☐☐
_____ protein ☐☐☐☐
Snack: _____ carbs ☐☐☐☐☐
Dinner: _____ healthy fats ☐☐☐☐
_____ soft drinks ___ coffee___
_____ Sleep # hours _____
Snack: _____ Vitamins Yes ☐ No ☐
Discretionary Calories:
  Fast food ☐☐☐☐☐   Sweets ☐☐☐☐☐
  Junk food ☐☐☐☐☐   Other ☐☐☐☐☐

Success requires that you push your body beyond your comfort zone!

Saturday water ☐☐☐☐☐☐☐☐
Breakfast: _____ dairy ☐☐☐☐☐
_____ veggies ☐☐☐☐☐
Lunch: _____ fruit ☐☐☐☐☐
_____ protein ☐☐☐☐
Snack: _____ carbs ☐☐☐☐☐
Dinner: _____ healthy fats ☐☐☐☐
_____ soft drinks ___ coffee___
_____ Sleep # hours ___
Snack: _____ Vitamins Yes ☐ No ☐
Discretionary Calories:
  Fast food ☐☐☐☐☐   Sweets ☐☐☐☐☐
  Junk food ☐☐☐☐☐   Other ☐☐☐☐☐

Sunday water ☐☐☐☐☐☐☐☐
Breakfast: _____ dairy ☐☐☐☐☐
_____ veggies ☐☐☐☐☐
Lunch: _____ fruit ☐☐☐☐☐
_____ protein ☐☐☐☐
Snack: _____ carbs ☐☐☐☐☐
Dinner: _____ healthy fats ☐☐☐☐
_____ soft drinks ___ coffee___
_____ Sleep # hours _____
Snack: _____ Vitamins Yes ☐ No ☐
Discretionary Calories:
  Fast food ☐☐☐☐☐   Sweets ☐☐☐☐☐
  Junk food ☐☐☐☐☐   Other ☐☐☐☐☐

Do you feel like you are making progress on your fitness goals?
Why or why not?

What could you do today to move you closer to your goals?

Distance Challenge Miles = _____

Week #9 Name_____

Strength Training Log

Exercises	Date	Date	Exercises	Date	Date
Chest			Arms		
Back			Core		
Shoulders			Legs/Glutes		

Cardio Log

	Cardio	#	Intensity	#
	Exercise	Mins	Level	Miles
Mon				
Tue				
Wed				
Thur				
Fri				
Sat				
Sun				
	Total Minutes ____		Total Miles ____	

Nutrition Goal for this week:

_____

Exercise Goal for this week:

_____

© 2009 Betty Kern. Please don't make illegal copies of this page

Other Exercise:

Distance Challenge Miles = _____

Week 10

Monday water ☐☐☐☐☐☐☐☐
- Breakfast: _____ dairy ☐☐☐☐☐
- _____ veggies ☐☐☐☐☐☐
- Lunch: _____ fruit ☐☐☐☐☐☐
- _____ protein ☐☐☐☐
- Snack: _____ carbs ☐☐☐☐☐☐
- Dinner: _____ healthy fats ☐☐☐☐
- _____ soft drinks __ coffee__
- _____ Sleep # hours _____
- Snack: _____ Vitamins Yes ☐ No ☐
- Discretionary Calories:
  - Fast food ☐☐☐☐☐   Sweets ☐☐☐☐☐
  - Junk food ☐☐☐☐☐   Other ☐☐☐☐☐

Tuesday water ☐☐☐☐☐☐☐☐
- Breakfast: _____ dairy ☐☐☐☐☐
- _____ veggies ☐ ☐☐☐☐☐
- Lunch: _____ fruit☐ ☐☐☐☐☐
- _____ protein☐ ☐☐☐
- Snack: _____ carbs ☐☐☐☐☐☐
- Dinner: _____ healthy fats☐ ☐☐☐
- _____ soft drinks__ coffee_
- _____ Sleep # hours _____
- Snack: _____ Vitamins Yes ☐ No ☐
- Discretionary Calories:
  - Fast food ☐☐☐☐☐   Sweets ☐☐☐☐☐
  - Junk food ☐☐☐☐☐   Other ☐☐☐☐☐

FITNESS TESTING RESULTS

Test	
Height	
Weight	
BMI	
% Body Fat	
Resting Heart Rate	
Aerobic Test	
Waist Circumference	

Wednesday water ☐☐☐☐☐☐☐☐☐
- Breakfast: _____ dairy ☐☐☐☐☐
- _____ veggies ☐☐☐☐☐
- Lunch: _____ fruit ☐☐☐☐☐
- _____ protein ☐☐☐☐
- Snack: _____ carbs ☐☐☐☐☐☐
- Dinner: _____ healthy fats ☐☐☐☐
- _____ soft drinks __ coffee__
- _____ Sleep # hours _____
- Snack: _____ Vitamins Yes ☐ No ☐
- Discretionary Calories:
  - Fast food ☐☐☐☐☐   Sweets ☐☐☐☐☐
  - Junk food ☐☐☐☐☐   Other ☐☐☐☐☐

Thursday water ☐☐☐☐☐☐☐☐☐
- Breakfast: _____ dairy ☐☐☐☐☐
- _____ veggies ☐☐☐☐☐
- Lunch: _____ fruit ☐☐☐☐☐
- _____ protein ☐☐☐☐
- Snack: _____ carbs ☐☐☐☐☐☐
- Dinner: _____ healthy fats ☐☐☐☐
- _____ soft drinks __ coffee__
- _____ Sleep # hours _____
- Snack: _____ Vitamins Yes ☐ No ☐
- Discretionary Calories:
  - Fast food ☐☐☐☐☐   Sweets ☐☐☐☐☐
  - Junk food ☐☐☐☐☐   Other ☐☐☐☐☐

Friday water ☐☐☐☐☐☐☐☐
- Breakfast: _____ dairy ☐☐☐☐☐
- _____ veggies ☐☐☐☐☐
- Lunch: _____ fruit ☐☐☐☐☐☐
- _____ protein ☐☐☐☐
- Snack: _____ carbs ☐☐☐☐☐☐
- Dinner: _____ healthy fats ☐☐☐☐
- _____ soft drinks __ coffee__
- _____ Sleep # hours _____
- Snack: _____ Vitamins Yes ☐ No ☐
- Discretionary Calories:
  - Fast food ☐☐☐☐☐   Sweets ☐☐☐☐☐
  - Junk food ☐☐☐☐☐   Other ☐☐☐☐☐

> "Your success and happiness lie within you."
> Helen Keller

Saturday water ☐☐☐☐☐☐☐☐☐
- Breakfast: _____ dairy ☐☐☐☐☐
- _____ veggies ☐☐☐☐☐
- Lunch: _____ fruit ☐☐☐☐☐☐
- _____ protein ☐☐☐☐
- Snack: _____ carbs ☐☐☐☐☐☐
- Dinner: _____ healthy fats ☐☐☐☐
- _____ soft drinks __ coffee__
- _____ Sleep # hours ____
- Snack: _____ Vitamins Yes ☐ No ☐
- Discretionary Calories:
  - Fast food ☐☐☐☐☐   Sweets ☐☐☐☐☐
  - Junk food ☐☐☐☐☐   Other ☐☐☐☐☐

Sunday water ☐☐☐☐☐☐☐☐☐
- Breakfast: _____ dairy ☐☐☐☐☐☐
- _____ veggies ☐☐☐☐☐
- Lunch: _____ fruit ☐☐☐☐☐☐
- _____ protein ☐☐☐☐
- Snack: _____ carbs ☐☐☐☐☐☐
- Dinner: _____ healthy fats ☐☐☐☐
- _____ soft drinks __ coffee__
- _____ Sleep # hours _____
- Snack: _____ Vitamins Yes ☐ No ☐
- Discretionary Calories:
  - Fast food ☐☐☐☐☐   Sweets ☐☐☐☐☐
  - Junk food ☐☐☐☐☐   Other ☐☐☐☐☐

Congratulations on completing the first quarter of this class!
You have made important steps toward a lifetime of health and wellness!
Believe in yourself!
You can accomplish anything…never give up!

Total Distance Challenge Miles = _____
Did you meet your goal?

Week #10

Name_____

Strength Training Log

Exercises	Date	Date	Exercises	Date	Date
Chest			Arms		
Back			Core		
Shoulders			Legs/Glutes		

Cardio Log

	Cardio Exercise	# Mins	Intensity Level	# Miles
Mon				
Tue				
Wed				
Thur				
Fri				
Sat				
Sun				
	Total Minutes _____		Total Miles	_____

Nutrition Goal for this week:

_____

Exercise Goal for this week:

_____

© 2009 Betty Kern. Please don't make illegal copies of this page

Other Exercise:

Total Distance Challenge Miles = _____

At the end of the first quarter...

Are you happy with the progress you made during the first quarter?

Why or why not?

What do you think _you_ could do differently in the second quarter to achieve your goals?

What could _we_ do differently in class that might help you achieve your goals?

How are you doing following your "good nutrition" plan?

What could you do to improve your eating habits?

2nd Quarter

Go for your goals!

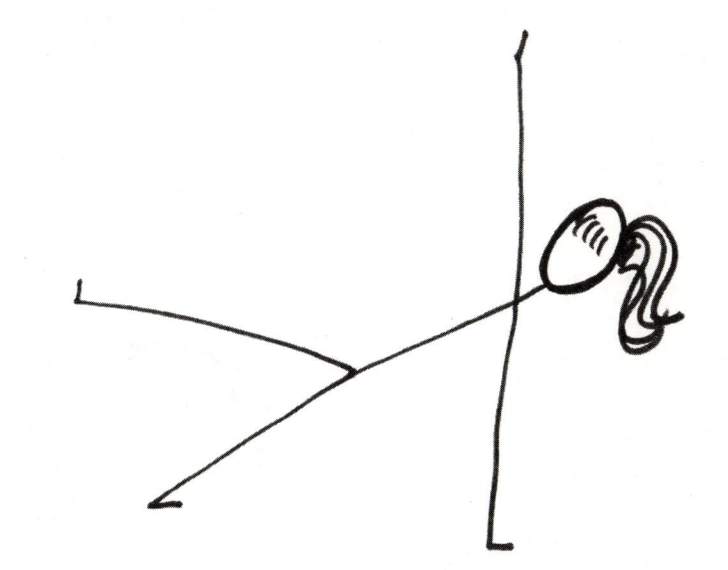

AB & PUSH-UP CHALLENGE

What?
Complete abdominal exercises and/or push-ups
& record the number you do in your journal

When??
_____ through _____

Where??
In class or at home!

Challenge Levels

ABS
Level 1: 50/day = 350/week
Level 2: 100/day = 700/week
Level 3: 200/day = 1400/week

Push-ups
Level 1: 10/day = 70/week
Level 2: 20/day = 140/week
Level 3: 30/day = 210/week

Lifestyle Evaluations

The following lifestyle evaluations will give you a picture of your current strengths and weaknesses in four categories: perspective/motivation, fat management, nutrition, and fitness. Take your time in responding to the evaluations and base your answers on your current attitudes or behavior. A special thanks to Danna Demetre for allowing us to use evaluations # 2, #3, & #4 taken from her book, <u>Scale Down</u>. To view her book and other resources go to <u>www.dannademetre.com</u>.

- Rate yourself on your first impression
- Don't go back and readjust your answers if you don't like your score
- Remember that this is a reality check. Just face the truth and move on!

Lifestyle Evaluation #1 – Perspective/Motivation

Pplease rate yourself (0 – Almost never; 1 – Sometimes; 2 – Often; 3 – Always)

_____ I see myself as a valued, unique individual.
_____ My choices and actions are morally responsible.
_____ I am thankful for the body given to me.
_____ My lifestyle habits are honorable to others and myself.
_____ I take responsibility for my body's size, shape and health.
_____ My attitude is this: I am not the center of the universe and I have a responsibility to help others.
_____ I understand that I have weaknesses and can overcome them with help.
_____ My personal goals are realistic and honorable.
_____ I take realistic steps toward my goals each day.
_____ I know that with consistent, healthy habits I can have a lean, healthy body.
_____ I am aware of the lies I believe about my body, looks, and health.
_____ I recognize and choose not to accept this negative thinking.
_____ I focus on the positive and strive to overcome obstacles in life.
_____ I am a work in progress and I benefit from each positive/healthy step I take.
_____ Everyday, I choose to make decisions that benefit my mind, body, attitude, health, family & relationships.
_____ Everyday, I strive to resist temptations that threaten to chip away at my dreams and goals.

_____ Add the total of all scores.

Scoring
- 40-48 Excellent! You have a good perspective.
- 31-39 Good. Your perspective is usually working for you.
- 22-30 Fair. It's time to get a new focus...the truth!
- < 21   Alert! Alert! Change your perspective now!

Lifestyle Evaluation #2 – Food Attitude Management

Please rate yourself (0 – Almost never; 1 – Sometimes; 2 – Often; 3 – Always)

_____   I feel in control of my food choices.

_____   I measure my size by how I look and feel, not the scale.

_____   I eat only when I'm hungry.

_____   I stop eating when I'm full.

_____   I understand why calories count.

_____   I eat four to five small meals or snacks per day.

_____   I limit my junk food, fast food, and desserts to less than 15% of my diet.

_____   I am happy with my body weight.

_____   I am happy with my size and shape.

_____   I can enjoy "fun food" without feeling guilty.

_____   I think about food only when I'm hungry.

_____   I can see myself eating and living in control.

_____   I walk or get purposeful exercise at least four times per week.

_____   I am very aware of my choices and how they affect my body.

_____   I say no to the latest diets or supplements promising quick results.

_____   I know if I'm going to be lean, I have to take daily action.

_____   Add the total of all scores.

Scoring

40-48   Excellent! You have a lean lifestyle.

31-39   Good. You're doing most things right!

22-30   Fair. It's time to take action.

< 21   Poor. Start with one step at a time

Lifestyle Evaluation #3 – Nutrition

Please rate yourself (0 – Almost never; 1- Sometimes; 2 – Often; 3 – Always)

_____ I think about what I eat and how it impacts my health.
_____ I have high energy to do all the things I want and need to do.
_____ I read labels and choose many foods based on that information
_____ I eat two to three servings of fruit each day.
_____ I eat three to four servings of vegetables each day.
_____ I choose whole-grain products over more processed foods.
_____ I know how much fiber I'm eating daily.
_____ I drink ten to twelve glasses of water daily.
_____ I eat breakfast every day.
_____ I eat a good source of protein with my breakfast.
_____ I choose and eat lean protein with my lunch.
_____ I limit my empty calories to less than 15% of my total diet.
_____ I limit caffeine and other stimulants, such as over-the-counter diet aids, and energy drinks.
_____ I take a multivitamin supplement daily.
_____ I take an antioxidant supplement daily.
_____ I choose "healthy" fats in my diet such as flaxseed oil, fish oils, olive oil, or canola oil.

_____ Add the total of all scores.

Scoring

40-48 Excellent! Your body loves you!
31-39 Good. You're on the right track.
22-30 Fair. It's time to try a little more high-octane fuel.
<21   Poor. Your body is crying, "Help!"

Lifestyle Evaluation #4 – Fitness

Please rate yourself (0 – Almost never; 1- Sometimes; 2 – Often; 3 – Always)

_____ I crave activity and find ways to move more each day.
_____ I enjoy exercise and how it makes my body feel.
_____ I have high energy to do all the things I want and need to do.
_____ I make exercise and activity a priority in my life.
_____ I understand the need for aerobic, strength, and flexibility training.
_____ I take the stairs or park far away whenever I can.
_____ I monitor my heart rate and know I am exercising safely.
_____ I am injury free and able to engage in most activities.
_____ Being healthy and fit is important to me.
_____ I listen to my body and know what it needs.
_____ I wear appropriate and quality shoes for exercise.
_____ I have a very active life and am moving throughout the day.
_____ I work out my major muscle groups two to three times each week.
_____ I can easily touch my toes without bending my knees.
_____ I maintain strong abdominal muscles.

_____ Add the total of all scores.

Scoring	
40-48	Excellent! You're a fit machine!
31-39	Good. Stay consistent.
22-30	Fair. Use it or lose it!
< 21	Poor. Take one small step and start moving!

Now that you've evaluated your lifestyle and identified your areas that need improvement, you can begin to take some steps to improve those areas and your health. Don't try to change everything at once! Small, step-by-step, consistent changes made over time will add up to a healthier you! You will learn information and tips to help you during this class and through this journal. Ask questions and ask for help when you need it!
Good luck as you begin your journey to a healthier lifestyle!

Lifestyle Evaluations

Name_____

1. Look back at your lifestyle evaluations. In general, what do the evaluations (scores) say about you?

    Lifestyle Evaluation #1 Perspective/Motivation:

    Lifestyle Evaluation #2 Food Attitude:

    Lifestyle Evaluation #3 Nutrition:

    Lifestyle Evaluation #4 Fitness:

2. What areas are your strengths?

3. What areas need improvement?

4. After completing the evaluation can you come up with at least three things you can do to improve the area(s) you listed in question #3?

Looking Back & Goal Setting
What have you learned so far?

Name _____

Nutrition – Look back at your "requirements" from the Food Guide Pyramid...page 25

Grains	Fruits	Vegetables	Milk	Meat & Beans
_____oz	_____cups	_____cups	_____cups	_____oz
_____ servings	_____ servings	_____ servings	_____ servings	_____ servings

Physical Activity – What is the recommended minutes of exercise/physical activity for teen girls each day?

SO HERE'S THE QUESTION...HOW ARE YOU DOING?

ARE YOU MEETING YOUR NUTRITION REQUIREMENTS EACH DAY? ARE YOU DRINKING ENOUGH WATER?

ARE YOU PHYSICALLY ACTIVE FOR THE RECOMMENDED AMOUNT OF TIME MOST DAYS OF THE WEEK?

IF YOU ARE MEETING YOUR NUTRITION AND EXERCISE RECOMMENDATIONS EACH DAY...**CONGRATULATIONS!**
IF YOU ARE NOT...HERE IS THE BIG QUESTION...**WHY NOT? WHAT IS HOLDING YOU BACK?**

Let's list some of the "things" that kept you or others in the class from meeting the nutrition and exercise recommendations?

What would help you keep on track with good nutrition and exercise habits?

GOALS!   Setting goals can help you keep focused! You probably **wanted** to get in the recommended number of minutes of exercise each day and to eat something from each of the food groups...but...for some reason **it just didn't happen**.

Or maybe you started out well and gradually slipped in your habits. So...this is where setting more specific goals or working strategies into your routine can help you be successful!

Setting specific daily goals/strategies that work into your schedule will greatly increase your chance for success!

For example, to increase the amount of water you drink each day, start the day off with a glass of water before you do anything else! To get in a little more exercise...before you get in the shower each day do 50 squats, 25 lunges, 50 sit-ups or 20 push-ups. To increase the number of vegetables or fruit in your diet, include one at lunch and dinner every day! Or if you know you cannot resist chocolate chip cookies...don't have any in the house! To stick to your workouts...you might need to make a "schedule" for working out for the week so you have specific activities for each day planned out ahead of time. Think about what will help you be successful! The goals/strategies need to be **specific** and include **daily, weekly**, and **longer** term goals!

**"You need strategies in place so you don't have to depend on willpower.
Willpower doesn't work anyway, because it fizzles out and you're back where you started,"
says Jay McGraw,** author of <u>The Ultimate Weight Solution for Teens</u>.

LET'S TALK A LITTLE MORE ABOUT GOALS!

As you think about setting goals to help you adopt a healthier lifestyle, there are a few things to keep in mind.

1) Goals will be easier to follow if you make them **specific and measureable**.   A goal to "get in better shape" is not measureable or specific. A more specific goal would be to improve your mile time from 12 minutes to 10 minutes.
2) Goals also need to include a **time-line and be reasonable**. So the goal to improve your mile time needs to include a date by which you will run that improved time. The goal must also be reasonable...in other words you should give yourself enough time to achieve the goal. If you are not sure what is reasonable, ask your teacher to help you set a time-line for achieving your goal!
3) Goals must also include things that are **within your control**. So if your goal is to run on the days you get off work early...what happens if your boss never lets you off early? You need to decide on a time to run that is not dependent on someone else's actions.
4) Goals should include a **strategy and steps** that will help you be successful! To improve that mile time your strategy could be to gradually increase your running time and/or speed each time you run. The steps could specify two days a week running a little father and three days a week trying to increase your speed at a shorter distance.
5) Lastly, goals need to include an **accountability factor**! In other words, you need to have someone either checking up on your progress or working out with you to help keep you on track!

Successfully following your goals will be easier if you structure them along the guidelines listed above!
- Take a moment to think about what your lifestyle evaluations said along with the goals you set at the beginning of this class.
- Think about your eating habits...do they have room for improvement?
- Think about your physical activity habits (aka exercise)...do they have room for improvement?
- Think about your study habits...do they have room for improvement?
- Think about your self-talk habits...do they have room for improvement?

GOALS

Name _____

Let's set some new goals for this quarter to help you get in the best shape of your life!

Make the goals specific, measureable, reasonable, within your control, include a time-line, strategies, steps and an accountability factor!

	Daily/Weekly Goal	Strategy/Steps	Time-line	Accountability?
Nutrition Goal				
Exercise Goal				
Study Habits Goal				
Sleep Goal				
Self-Talk/Attitude Goal				

Self-Image & Body-Image...
Let's see what you think!

Name _____

Define self-image:

What does "ideal" self-image mean?

Do you think most people live up to their "ideal" self-image?

For you...is there a big difference between how you see yourself and how you'd like to be?

Could that be a problem?

Define body-image:

What does "ideal" body image mean?

Do you think most people live up to their "ideal" body image?

For you...is there a big difference between how you see yourself and how you'd like to be?

Could that be a problem?

Can someone have a good self-image and a bad body image?

How or why?

93

Can someone have a good body-image and a bad self-image?

How or why?

Do you have a good self-image?

List some things that affect a person's self-image....positive & negative:

List some things that affect a person's body-image...positive & negative:

Do you have a good body-image?

What is a negative self-image?

How can a negative self-image or body-image impact a person's life?

Do you think a person's self-image/body-image affects how you see that person? How? Why?

Have you ever met a beautiful person who lacked self-confidence?

Why do you think that happens?

Have you ever met someone whose personality made him/her more attractive?

How does that work?

Are all beautiful people happy?

Why do you think that?

Do you think if you could change two things that you do not like about yourself, then you would be happy?

Why or why not?

Research shows that if you change those "two things." That you probably would not be happier!

Do you think that is true? Why?

What would make you truly happy?
Be honest!

What are 5 qualities that you most admire in others your age?

What are 5 qualities that you most admire in a role model older than you?

Do you possess any of the qualities you most admire in others?

What could you do to develop these qualities?

Are these qualities based mostly on appearance or character/personality/career?

If they are appearance related, can you realistically get there?

If yes…what can you do to move in that direction?

If the qualities were character/personality/career related, how can you acquire these qualities?

What do you think is the most important thing you can do to improve your self-image and body-image?

*"Always be a first-rate version of yourself,
instead of a second-rate version of somebody else."*
Judy Garland, Singer-Actress
Wizard of Oz

Healthy Image Boosters

i. **Know Yourself**...accept your strengths and weaknesses

ii. **View media with a critical eye**...remember that all photos have been "enhanced"

iii. **Ask for and accept help**...don't be too proud to get the help you need

iv. **Give yourself a break**...nobody is perfect...don't beat yourself up

v. **Be true to you**...be yourself, trust yourself and your abilities

vi. **Control self talk**...quit comparing yourself to everyone else, change negative self-talk to positive self-talk

vii. **Take a break**...take time to rest, relax and get away from the stresses of life

viii. **Get & stay active**...find an activity that you love to do and make it part of your daily routine...or change things up daily...just make a commitment to get moving daily!

ix. **Understand you are more than your body**...value your mind and talents

x. **Build a better body image**...work on accepting yourself as you are or making & following a plan to change the changeable things

Body Type/Design

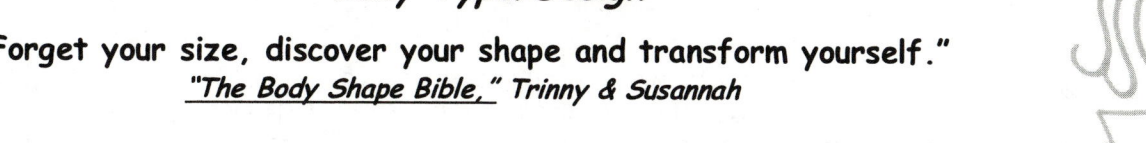

"Forget your size, discover your shape and transform yourself."
"The Body Shape Bible," Trinny & Susannah

It's all about balance. The experts agree! Just as you need to have balance in all of the dimensions of your life for things to go smoothly and to feel your best. Clinton Kelly and Stacy London's book <u>Dress Your Best</u> says "the key to looking your best is to create a balanced body shape through clothing." Clinton and Stacy also recommend dressing your body as it is right now! Your goal may be to lose weight or to get more toned…and that is great. However, dressing to look your best along the way will boost your confidence and help motivate you to achieve your goals! Plus, you may get some unexpected compliments…wouldn't that be nice!

Body Type/Design

- You will probably not find an exact match for your body type…you may tend towards one type but have some characteristics from another
- You can use the body type definitions as a starting point…let the basic recommendations for the style and fit of clothing guide you to finding what looks best on <u>your</u> body
- You may need to use some guidelines from more than one body type to help you dress your best…be careful…some body types are not compatible…ask for help if you are having trouble determining your body type
- You can break some of the "rules" for a particular body type and get away with it if you have a particularly strong feature to accentuate…don't be afraid to ask a trusted friend if your outfit "works" for you

Stacy London, co-host of TLC's "What Not to Wear" gives five tips for looking your best in the August 2008 edition of <u>People: Style Watch</u> magazine:

1) **Know yourself**: "Accept your body type for what it is". Embrace your size and find what works for you.

2) **Fit is key**: Once you have found the cuts that flatter your body type, **have your clothes altered** for perfect fit.

3) **Don't fall back on black**: Other colors, like navy, charcoal grey and chocolate brown are also slimming. Also, cut is more important than color.

4) **Ignore labels**: Brand and size labels are secondary. The fit of the garment is the important thing.

5) **Good posture is essential**: "Stand with your shoulders back, chest out and tummy in."

Determining Your Body Type/Design

To determine your body type stand in front of a full length mirror in your underwear...look at your proportions including your shoulders, chest, waist, hips, height, legs and even your rear-end! Remember, you probably will not "fit" exactly into one body type...that's o.k. Find the one that best matches your body and use the recommendations for that body type to dress your best!

Body Types/Designs

Fashion design experts give various names to the different body types. Basically they fall into the six categories below.
The body type definitions below have been taken from the book _Dress Your Best_ by Clinton Kelly & Stacy London.

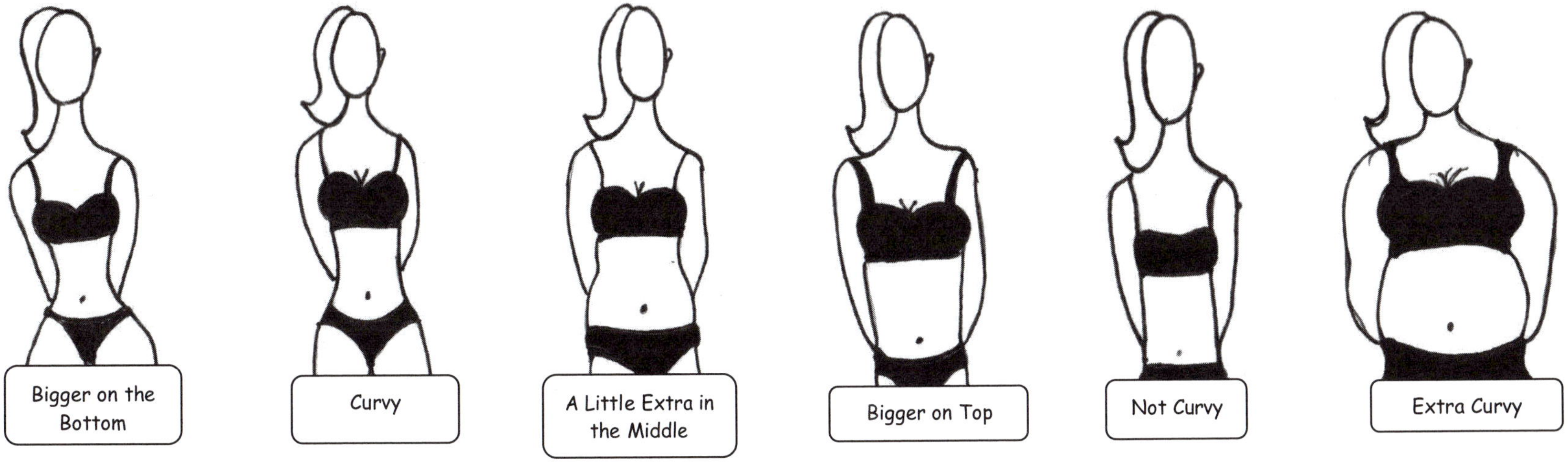

| Bigger on the Bottom | Curvy | A Little Extra in the Middle | Bigger on Top | Not Curvy | Extra Curvy |

There is no one perfect body!
We have to learn to accept our unique body and celebrate its strengths & weaknesses.
Improve and work on the areas that can be changed and recognize/accept what cannot be changed.

Basic Recommendations from the experts:

Bigger on the Bottom (pear): Draw attention away from your lower body to balance out your look.

- ✓ Wear a well-fitting, supportive bra
- ✓ Wear shirts and jackets that fit to show off your waist and define your upper body...keep them above your hips...you don't want to make your lower body look shorter!
- ✓ Wear v-neck tops and tops with interesting details. Layering tops of different lengths will attract attention upwards and add volume.
- ✓ Wear pants that are free of detail and absolutely no pleats! A mid-rise pant/jean is recommended.
- ✓ Wear dresses that are A-line or "fit & flare" which are fitted through the waist and flare out to the hemline.

Curvy (hourglass): Define your waist and elongating your legs will balance out your look!
- ✓ Wear clothes that follow your curves and show off your narrow waist.
- ✓ Wear simple and smooth tops that show off your curves…wrap tops work well for you!
- ✓ Wear flat front, low-waist, flare pants or jeans…don't wear super-low-rise pants…they will draw attention to your hips and give you love handles!
- ✓ Wear dresses…you look great in them! All types look great on you but avoid straight tunic style and shapeless dresses…they hide your curves!

A Little Extra in the Middle (apple): Proportion out your midsection to balance out your look!
- ✓ Wear layers…stretch wrap tops over fine knit tops…the wrap tops create curves or a "V-shape."
- ✓ Wear the longer tees with a sweater, short cut jacket or shrug over them…this create a slimming look
- ✓ Wear your tops un-tucked and avoid fabrics that cling to every bulge as well as crop tops!
- ✓ Wear flat front, semi-low rise, boot cut or flared jeans or pants with some stretch to them…avoid pleated or gathered bottoms…keep the waist line flat as possible!
- ✓ Wear knee length dresses with straighter lines to elongate your body and skim over the curves of your upper body and show off your legs!

Bigger on Top (inverted triangle): Add some volume to your lower half to balance out your look!
- ✓ Wear a bra with good support!!
- ✓ Wear tops in soft fabrics with v-necks or knit tops with u-necklines to help define your waist…soft collarless tunics work great for you!
- ✓ Wear layers with something soft and feminine underneath to add shape.
- ✓ Wear tops with belts, ties and ribbons to add shape.
- ✓ Wear pants/jeans that are boot-cut or flare…cargo pants work great for you to add volume to your lower half!
- ✓ Wear shift dresses, tunic dresses or soft dresses with a v-neck ruffle.

Not Curvy (rectangle): Defining your waist and creating curves will help balance out your look!
- ✓ Wear clingy clothes to help create curves…knit tops and boy-cut pants/jeans.
- ✓ Wear capped sleeved tees and tank tops to show off your well-defined arms!
- ✓ Wear high necklines or v-necks that are not too low or wear a tank or tee underneath…show off your back or arms rather than your lack of cleavage!
- ✓ Wear tops or dresses that have extra "frills" that will add volume to your upper half!
- ✓ Wear fitted clothes…you will get lost in clothes that are too big!
- ✓ Wear flat front, semi low rise, hip skimming boot cuts…you can wear well fitting jeans/pants to help create curves…just not too tight…you can also add detail to the pockets, etc.
- ✓ Pencil skirts with a blouse tucked in will help create curves…add a belt for more even shape.

Extra Curvy: Elongate your shape to help balance out your look!
- ✓ Wear clothing with straight lines and flattering seaming.
- ✓ Wear stiffer fabrics rather than too much ruffle and frill.
- ✓ Wear leather or other heavy material jacket that sits at the top of the hips.
- ✓ Wear clothing that does not add weight to your look…go easy on added extras.
- ✓ Wear clothing that fits…don't get lost in clothing that is too big…it doesn't hide your weight…it make you look heavier!
- ✓ Wear wider-leg jeans to help balance the body.

Body Type, Fashion and You!

Name _____

What about eyes, skin tone/color and hair color? Should these influence your clothing choices? What if you have fabulous blue eyes or exquisite deep brown eyes...? What if you have amazing auburn hair, gorgeous dark brown or striking blond hair...? What if you have beautiful brown skin or lovely ivory skin...?

Yes...you should consider these when choosing your clothing! Bring out your eye color with a top that matches! Wear clothing that flatters you skin tone! Bring out the beauty in your tresses with colors that complement your hair color.

What body type most closely matches yours?

Do you lean a little towards another body type as well?

List three of your positive physical characteristics...yes, you have at least three!

1) _____

2) _____

3) _____

How can you dress to accentuate these in a modest, attractive and appropriate fashion?

1) _____

2) _____

3) _____

From the guidelines listed on the previous pages, do you think all styles look good on everybody?

Should you or can you still wear something that is not recommended for your body type?

If you are dressing for a really important event, would <u>you</u> follow the recommendations of the experts? Why?

What are some of the fashion guidelines that you could put into practice to help you look your best?

Do you have any items that you usually wear that do not complement your body shape from what you have learned?

Obviously, you cannot replace all of your clothes…even the ones that don't "work" for you…
Adjusting or changing your style needs to be a gradually process as you can afford it!

There is no one perfect body!
We have to learn to accept our unique body and celebrate its strengths & weaknesses.
Improve and work on the areas that can be changed and recognize/accept what cannot be changed.

Do all of the girls in your class think the same guys are good-looking?

What do you think makes a guy attractive?

Did you know that guys will give a variety of answers when asked what makes a girl attractive? Not all guys are looking for the same physical characteristic in girls…isn't that good news?

What do you think about that?

Body-Type & Fashion Assignment

Name _____

Determine the body type/design that *most closely* matches your body from the six types below.
Remember you may have characteristics from more than one body type!

Bigger on Bottom	Curvy	A Little Extra in the Middle	Bigger on Top	Not Curvy	Extra Curvy

→ Use resources including books, magazines, and websites to design two outfits for school, one for a social event, one for casual wear and one for a dance or dress-up event (church, wedding, etc.)

→ Choose a swim suit that would be best for your body.

→ Draw and color your outfit for each occasion or find pictures of your outfit!

→ Use a poster board to display your fashion choices!

→ Think about not only the styles but also the types of material/fabric/prints as well as where and when you will wear these outfits.

→ Think about your physical characteristics that you listed to accentuate with fashion...modestly & appropriately!

→ Find accessories that will finish your look! Don't forget the shoes!

→ Make a list of at least 12 "essentials" that <u>you</u> think every wardrobe needs!

THIS PROJECT IS DUE _____

Eating Disorders

Food…isn't it interesting how Americans have such crazy relationships with food?
On one extreme we have people who don't think twice about what they put into their bodies and
on the other extreme we have people who obsess about every morsel they consume!
Neither one of these extremes is healthy!
Food is fuel for the body. The better the fuel consumed, the healthier the body.
Obviously, food is meant to be enjoyed…look at the bounty of delicious food in nature…fruits, vegetables, nuts, etc!
The problem in our culture is that food is often consumed for pleasure only and little thought is given to nutritional impact or
the damaging effects of certain foods on the body.
Everything in our culture revolves around food…did you ever notice that? Do you think this is a problem?
Our cultural relationship with food can be a problem for people with certain medical conditions that restrict the types of food they can consume as well as for
people with eating disorders. What are eating disorders and how do they develop?

Eating Disorders – are patterns of eating that are characterized by abnormal eating habits and a distorted view of food and body weight and/or size. These habits regularly ignore hunger and satiety signals often resulting in either eating when not hungry or not eating when hungry. Eating disorders include **anorexia**, **bulimia**, **binge eating disorder (BED)**, and **eating disorders not otherwise specified**. Common characteristics among people with various eating disorders includes: low self-esteem, a need for distraction, feelings of emptiness, perfectionism, a desire to be respected or admired, a need to control, and difficulty expressing feelings. Eating disorders are present in women of various size, shape and weight from very thin to extremely overweight.

Anorexia:

- occurs in all social classes
- intense fear of gaining weight or becoming "fat"
- pursues thinness unrealistically
- feel as if they cannot control certain elements in their life
- weight loss of more than 15% of ideal body weight
- voluntary refusal to eat
- absence of at least three consecutive menstrual cycles
- often a perfectionist with unrealistic goals

Risk factors for Anorexia

- poor body-image
- poor self-image
- athlete or dancer
- teasing by peers or family
- high body fat
- discomfort discussing problems with parents
- pear-shaped body
- maternal preoccupation with diets

Symptoms and Medical Complications of Anorexia

- hair, nail and skin problems
- amenorrhea…loss of monthly cycle
- extreme sensitivity to cold temperatures
- body hair growth
- edema…swelling around the ankles
- unusual eating habits
- preoccupation with food, weight or calories
- extreme physical activity
- poor self-esteem
- social isolation
- denial of problem
- cardiac dysfunction…heart problems
- gastrointestinal difficulties
- structural abnormalities of the brain
- growth retardation
- delay of puberty or interruption
- reduced peak bone mass
- episodes of hypoglycemia
- elevated cholesterol
- thyroid problems
- concentration problems
- injuries to nerves and tendons
- nervousness at mealtimes…especially around others
- excessive studying or working

*"Anorexia is like you're running down a hill, and all this wind is going through your hair, and it's exciting.
But all of a sudden, you're going too fast and start to spiral out of control. You fall.
Then you're just sitting on the ground, shocked, with all these bruises."*
Amy's Story, <u>Girl's Life</u>, 2002

Bulimia:

- Often normal weight individual
- Binge eating episodes followed by self-induced vomiting, fasting, excessive exercise or use of laxatives or diuretics
- Similar to anorexia with an intense preoccupation with weight, dieting and food
- Goal is to attain the "ideal" body
- Chaotic eating pattern including specific rules about what to eat, when, where, how, etc.
- Feel out-of-control during binging episodes
- Purging brings initial relief but later guilt and shame take over
- Prefers not to eat in front of others
- Evaluates self-worth according to body shape and weight

Symptoms & Medical Complications of Bulimia

- Gastrointestinal problems
- Dental & gum problems
- Muscle cramps & weakness
- Fatigue
- Heart rhythm problems
- Dehydration & electrolyte imbalance
- Congestive heart failure
- Weight fluctuations
- Bloodshot eyes
- Esophagus damage
- Headaches
- Bloating
- Low weight even with eating lots of food
- Usually uses bathroom after eating
- Don't like to eat in front of others
- Excessive exercise
- Laxative & diuretic use
- Binge eating and purging at least twice a week for at least three months

*Anorexia and bulimia cause more deaths than any other psychiatric disorder!
Early identification and treatment are essential!*

Binge Eating Disorder (BED)

- Most common eating disorder
- Binge behavior without the purging or excessive exercise that characterizes bulimia
- Often obese
- Low self-esteem
- Disgusted with actions
- Depressed, feel guilty about actions
- Feels out of control while eating
- 30% of women who seek treatment to lose weight had BED

Eating Disorders Not Otherwise Specified
- Includes many eating disorders that don't exactly fit the "requirements" of the other categories
- Patients may meet most of the criteria for anorexia except they have not missed three consecutive menstrual periods
- Patients may be of normal weight and purge without bingeing
- Patient may not present medical complications but some medical concerns
- Many of the symptoms listed above may be seen but not to the same degree as someone with full blown anorexia or bulimia

"Eating disorders commonly occur in people with low self-esteem, they feel they are not "good enough." They believe that thinness will make them into better and almost perfect people. The truth is that a thinner body does not make a person better, just smaller. There is simply less of the person to love. The individual is the same person, just obsessed, withdrawn, and tired. And when someone severely restricts food, he or she loses muscle, strength and stamina."

Nancy Clark, *Nancy Clark's Sports Nutrition Guidebook*

What were they thinking?
In the beginning the girls said…
"It made me feel powerful that I could ignore their pleas and starve myself"
"A voice in my head kept telling me the less food I let touch my lips, the more stable and safe I would be"
"I felt I had finally found something I could completely control…my weight."

In the end the girls said…
"I suddenly realized how unfamiliar those feeling of joy had become to me. I wanted them back. I wanted to live."
"In many ways, my anorexia was an attempt to find out if my family, friends, and boyfriend would still love me even if I weren't perfect."
"I couldn't concentrate on lectures. I couldn't remember a thing I had read moments after reading it. Just climbing a set of stairs made my heart race. I was always exhausted."

Treatment for Eating Disorders
Teenagers with eating disorders need to be evaluated and treated by a team of professionals. The treatment will focus on the many aspects that have contributed to the development of an eating disorder including physical, emotional, family and social influences. The treatment team should include a medical doctor, a registered dietitian, a psychologist and a nurse that have experience helping patients with eating disorders. Families should be involved in the treatment and care of the patient because family issues are often involved in the disease process. Early intervention can help teenagers recover more quickly and avoid many health problems.

What should you do if you suspect a friend or family member has an eating disorder?
Share your concern with your friend or family member in a loving, nonjudgmental way. Convey the message that you are concerned about her health and only want the best for her! Be prepared for her to deny having a problem. Don't become confrontational…it will only push her away! Continue to be a good friend and talk about the situation again. Find an adult…teacher, parent, counselor…who can help monitor the situation. Be ready to seek out medical help, if necessary.

Most importantly, be supportive! Continue to be her friend even when the going gets rough!
Be creative in ways you deal with her! Don't give up on your friend or family member…she needs you!

Family, Friends & Relationships
Your relationships with family and friends have a greater impact on the quality of your life than all of the "things" that most of us consider essential.

<u>Relationships</u> – can be very complicated! Isn't that an understatement?
Why do <u>you</u> think that some relationships get so complicated? Take a minute or more and think about that question.

<u>Family Relationships & Friends</u> – ever wonder why our relationships with friends sometimes seem "easier" than with family?
Why do <u>you</u> think your relationships with friends often seem easier? Do <u>you</u> have any influence on this?

<u>Family</u> – even though we cannot control the actions of others in our family, we can control our reactions to them.
Often, if we react with kindness, we will get kindness in return. However, if we react with a negative or bad attitude, we will often get the same in return.
What do you think about that? If you have a difficult relationship in your family, do you think changing the way you deal with it would help?
Why or why not?

Have you ever noticed that members of the family seem to have different "roles" they play? One person may always seem to cheer everyone up while another keeps everyone focused during a project. Once you recognize that everyone has different strengths and weaknesses you can allow family members to fulfill various roles/jobs without passing judgment. This doesn't mean those daily chores or other menial jobs aren't shared but rather that you give family members a "break" when they don't do things exactly the way you want them done or see things the way you see them!

Think about your family relationships. Do any of them have room for improvement?

What could you do to help improve those relationships?

One of the best ways to show someone your love is to help him/her with something. Think of some ways that you could help family members... it doesn't have to be a "big deal" ...just offer some help or do something without being asked to do it! The amazing thing is this...as you help others in your family, they will in turn begin to look for ways to help you. A change occurs where you are now working together with a healthier attitude and everything goes smoother! Give it a try...at first your family may wonder what you are up to or what you want. But keep going and you will begin to see a transformation at least with someone in your family!
"My grandma used to say, **"You get more with honey than with that other stuff."** Guess what....she was right!
Make a difference in your family by treating everyone the way you would like to be treated...you may be surprised at the results" Betty Kern

Friends – what do your friendships say about you?

Are your friendships healthy? What does that mean? Do you have fun together, trust each other, encourage each other, cheer each other up, help each other, spend time together, agree to disagree but still be friends, talk about important stuff, defend each other, worry about each other, tease in a fun way, respect each other, talk about problems, include each other in special events, share your 'stuff', etc.

If you have friendships that look more like the opposite of what is described above, **they are not healthy**. Unhealthy friendships can harm you in various ways: lower self-esteem, affect your attitude, cause stress, encourage unhealthy behaviors, harm other relationships with family and other friends, discourage your interests and talents, to name a few.

Take a moment and think about your friendships.
Are all of your friendships healthy?

Are you being a good friend?

What do your parents think about these relationships?

Do all of your friends like each other? Why or why not and does that matter?

Never allow a friend or anyone else to make you feel unimportant or worthless. Don't be afraid to end a friendship or at least limit the time you spend with a friend who doesn't respect you or causes problems for you. Choose your friends wisely...they will help shape who you become!
Choose friend with similar interests. Look around... there may be someone who needs your friendship right now!

"Forgiveness is the oil of relationships." Josh McDowell

What about your boyfriend?

Do you have a healthy relationship?

Does he like your family?

Do you fight?

Does he like your friends?

Does he respect you?

Does he encourage your goals and dreams?

Does he respect your limits for intimacy?

Do your parents and friends like him?

If you answered no to any of these questions, then you should take some time to consider if this is a relationship that you should continue!

It is better to be alone than to be in a bad relationship! You are young! Many, many girls who stay in bad relationships end up getting married to that person and living in a bad marriage. You end up married to the wrong person by staying in or by becoming intimate with that person! Think, think, think...look at that person's family, friends, attitudes, habits, grades, etc., and make good decisions when you date!

Respect yourself enough to date a nice guy who respects and values you as a person as well as your goals and dreams!

Take a moment and make a list of qualities that you would want your future husband to possess.
Date guys that live up to your expectations!
Otherwise...you are likely to end up marrying a guy who does not possess those qualities either!
Think about all areas...physical, emotional, intellectual, and spiritual, etc!

Future husband or boyfriend qualities:

Exercise and Pregnancy

(FYI...THIS INFORMATION IS PROVIDED FOR FUTURE REFERENCE AND SHOULD NOT BE CONSIDERED ENCOURAGEMENT TO BECOME PREGNANT AT THIS TIME!)

Is it safe to exercise when you are pregnant?
Are there any benefits to participating in a fitness program while pregnant?

The answer to both questions is **YES!**

THE GOAL FOR EXERCISING DURING PREGNANCY IS TO MAINTAIN FITNESS!
It is very important to check with your doctor before beginning an exercise program during pregnancy!

Exercising during pregnancy has several benefits:

- helps control weight gain
- tones muscles
- improves posture
- combats insomnia
- increases circulation...controls swelling of the legs and ankles
- helps develop good breathing techniques
- helps you get back in shape faster after you deliver the baby...back to your pre-pregnancy weight
- keeps your energy level up
- helps build stamina needed for delivery and post-delivery recovery
- leads to an easier and shorter delivery and birth
- conditions the baby for the stress of labor and delivery
- helps a mother prepare mentally for labor and delivery
- gives one a feeling of control over her body during pregnancy
- conditions muscles that will play a major role in labor and delivery

Due to a shift in the center of gravity as pregnancy progresses, balance becomes a problem. Therefore, caution should be used in any exercise that requires balance.

Exercises for Pregnancy
Always check with your doctor first!
The most important thing is to choose an exercise that you enjoy and will continue with during your pregnancy.

Safe Exercises:
   *brisk walking
   *low-impact aerobics - no bouncing
   *stationary cycling
   *swimming or water aerobics
   *stretching or flexibility exercises
   *yoga (with some restrictions)

Acceptable Exercises:
   *cross-country skiing
   *golf
   *hiking
   *jogging
   *racket sports
   *weight training

High-Risk Activities:
   *downhill skiing
   *horseback riding
   *scuba diving
   *water skiing
   *sail boarding
   *Contact sports

109

Strength Training Exercises Recommended by the National Strength and Conditioning Association for Pregnancy (Feb '06):

*To help with increased weight of abdomen and chest during pregnancy:
- *Shoulder press
- *Lateral raises
- *Bent over lateral raises
- *Front Raises
- *Upright rows
- *Bent-over rows

*To help with labor and delivery:
- *Abductors/Adductors - legs exercises in four directions with bands
- *Hamstrings/Glutes/Quads - leg extension/curl machines, lunges, squats(for a while), warrior 1 & 2
- *Flexibility exercises!
- *Kegel exercises!!

Precautions and Guidelines
Consult with your doctor once you find out you are pregnant!!

Start Slowly. Listen to your body.

If you have been participating in a regular exercise program, you should be able to continue on the same level for the first trimester (12 weeks), provided you have no complications with your pregnancy. Even if you have not been exercising prior to becoming pregnant, you can begin to exercise slowly and actually become more fit during your pregnancy. It is important to monitor your heart rate and breathing during exercise. In general, your heart rate should not exceed 140 beats/minute. You should be able to carry on a conversation while you are exercising... if not, slow down.

Avoid exercising at extreme altitude or in a hot, humid environment.
In the summer, exercise in the early morning or late evening, not in the heat of the day.

Drink plenty of water!

As your pregnancy progresses, the intensity of your exercise should be reduced. You can continue to exercise just at a lower intensity level. Be careful not to over stretch... during pregnancy a hormone called relaxin is produced to induce hyper-flexibility in the joints and musculature, which allows for expansion of the uterus and the pelvic floor. In the last trimester, avoid ballistic movements, such as jumping or running.

Do Kegel exercises religiously.
Wear a good bra, preferably a sports bra especially during exercise.

Abdominal crunches performed in a supine position while pregnant could cause a tear in the rectus abdominis muscle.
After the first trimester, do not do any exercises while lying on your back.

Good nutrition is essential! Follow a healthy diet and include all food groups daily! Take your prenatal vitamins!
It is very important for all women of child-bearing age to take Folic Acid (a B vitamin).
Folic Acid has been shown to help prevent birth defects of the brain and spinal cord. It needs to be taken before conception and throughout pregnancy.
The March of Dimes recommends that all women should take a multi-vitamin that contains 400mcg of Folic Acid.

Effects of tobacco/alcohol/drugs on the developing baby!

Smoking – in general increases the risk of lung cancer, other lung disease and heart problems for the mother

During pregnancy smoking can harm both the baby and the mother.

- Doubles the risk of low-birth weight (< 5.5 lbs)
- Slows fetal growth
- Increases the risk of pre-term delivery
- Increase the risk of serious health problems as well as lifetime disabilities including cerebral palsy, mental retardation, learning disabilities & death
- Babies experience withdrawal-like symptoms at birth
- Babies are three times more likely to die from Sudden Infant Death Syndrome (SIDS)
- Pregnancy complications can include: Placenta Previa – a low lying placenta that covers part or all of the opening of the uterus; Placenta Abruption – the placenta peels away from the uterine wall before delivery…both conditions can cause heavy bleeding that can endanger the life of both the mother & baby
- Women who smoke anytime during the month before pregnancy to the end of the first trimester (12 weeks) are more likely to have a baby with birth defects including heart defects
- Smoking can also cause premature rupturing of the membrane – the sac that holds the baby – while still inside the uterus – often causing birth of a premature baby…once ruptured, labor and delivery will occur within a few hours

Alcohol - *Consuming alcohol during pregnancy can cause physical and mental birth defects!*

No level of alcohol use during pregnancy is safe! Even moderate or "light" drinking can harm the fetus!

Effects of alcohol on the baby: the alcohol passes swiftly through the placenta wall to the baby. Because the baby's body is immature, the alcohol is broken down more slowly which causes the blood alcohol level to be even higher than the mothers. The blood alcohol level will also remain elevated longer than the mother's potentially causing life-long damage and disabilities!

Alcohol & Birth Defects: birth defects can range from mild to severe! Mental retardation, learning, emotional and behavioral problems, defects affecting the heart, face and other organs, low birth weight, still birth, as well as, the most tragic birth defect "Fetal Alcohol Syndrome." The brain and other organs are developing as early as the third week of pregnancy and are very vulnerable to damage!

Fetal Alcohol Syndrome presents both mental and physical birth defects.

- **There is no cure for FAS**
- **Preventable birth defect**…but one of the most common causes of mental retardation!
- Babies with FAS:
  - Small at birth and usually don't ever catch up on growth
  - Poor coordination
  - Short attention span
  - Emotional and behavioral problems
  - Characteristic facial features including small eyes, thin upper lip, no groove between nose and upper lip
  - Organs don't form properly…especially the heart
  - Brain can be smaller and formed abnormally
  - Some degree of mental retardation is present

Breastfeeding and Alcohol consumption: small amounts of alcohol will pass through breast milk to the baby. This could affect motor skill development and cause other problems. The recommendation is to abstain from alcohol while breastfeeding your baby!

Illicit Drug Use During Pregnancy (in other words...illegal drugs!)

Includes marijuana, cocaine, Ecstacy, meth-amphetamines, speed, ice, crank, crystal meth, heroin, inhaling glue or solvents, and "club drugs" like PCP (angel dust), Ketamine (special K), and LSD (acid)

ALL OF THESE DRUGS CAN CAUSE SERIOUS BIRTH DEFECTS TO THE BABY! THESE PROBLEMS WILL NOT GO AWAY...MANY OF THE BIRTH DEFECTS WILL SERIOUSLY AFFECT THE QUALITY OF LIFE THAT THIS CHILD WILL HAVE FOREVER!

Birth defects from illicit drugs include: low birth weight, withdrawal symptoms (crying, trembling, jitteriness, breathing problems, unable to be comforted), heart defects, cleft lip/palate, learning difficulties, club foot, mental retardation, cerebral palsy, smaller heads (smaller brains), behavior problems, sudden infant death syndrome (SIDS), stroke, heart attack and even death!

Please don't make an innocent baby suffer...don't do drugs...especially when you are pregnant!

Think about your habits before you become pregnant.
Any habits that are unhealthy for you are even more harmful to the unborn baby!
Be responsible with your sexuality and protect not only your health but the health of your unborn child.

Healthy Living
Putting it all together!

We have "talked" about a lot of important life issues and concerns that impact every area of your life! How can you take what has been presented and apply it to your life?
Below are some final thoughts to help you put it all together!

I. *Healthy Eating..."you are what you eat!"* Yes this is an old cliché but it is so true!

- Eat foods that will nourish your body! **Food is fuel... the main purpose of food is to fuel your body!**
- Listen to your body and respond to its natural hunger signals.
- Eat foods that taste good but also are nutrient packed! Food for pleasure should be secondary!
- Remember...No food is off limits...you just have to limit those 'certain' foods.
- Go ahead and enjoy a treat now and then...just don't make it an everyday occurrence or keep the portion very small!
- Know your weaknesses...keep temptations at bay...set yourself up for success!
- Drink water and limit those high-calorie, sugar-laden drinks! **Water is so important!**
- Keep food in its proper perspective...don't let it have power over you...you are in control!
- Eat fresh, unprocessed foods as often as possible...limit boxed foods...they contain too much "bad stuff!"
- Balance out high fat choices with fruits and vegetables...work at meeting your Food Pyramid recommendations!
- Vary your food choices to improve the nutrition content of your diet and to keep you from getting bored!
- Be an example of healthy living to your family and friends by your food choices.
- Don't let mistakes completely ruin your plan! If you feel like you have blown your healthy eating plan, start making better choices the next time you eat!
- Employ the support of family and friends to help you eat healthier!

II. *Healthy Exercise...something is better than nothing! Get a daily dose of exercise!*

- Do the best you can to work towards the recommendation for teens ...60 minutes of physical activity every day!

- Include strength, flexibility and aerobic exercises!

- Do some sort of physical activity every day! Work it into your schedule!

- Find a friend to join you for a workout!

- Find an activity you enjoy...you are more likely to stick with it, if you like it!

- Be realistic in your expectations!

- Vary your workouts to prevent boredom and create a more balanced physique!

- Keep exercise in perspective...too much of a good thing can be bad! Don't overdo it!

III. **Healthy Thinking...focus on the positive!**

- Look at life situations with a balanced perspective

- Explore both the positive and negative parts of a situation...this will help keep upsetting or disappointing situations in perspective.

- Focus on the positive whenever possible!

- Replace negative self-talk with positive statements!

- Don't allow a comment from someone to steal your confidence! People will make mean, unkind, upsetting comments...you have to dismiss them! Only you can allow others to steal your joy!

- Keep a healthy perspective about your body. Resolve to improve the areas that are within your control and accept the things you cannot change. And remember...the media touches up all photos that you see in magazines and on the internet!

- Walk tall and with confidence...how others view you often is a reflection of your self-confidence!

- Remind yourself that weight and shape are not the only way to evaluate self-worth.

- Treat others with kindness and celebrate individual differences...everyone has gifts and special talents to share.

- Seek help if life's problems are overwhelming you! Find an adult who can help you!

- Enjoy life by keeping your attitude positive...you will be amazed the difference a positive attitude makes!

- Keep exercising to help your stress level and improve your mood!

- Believe in your ability to set and achieve goals! You can be successful! Go for your goals!

Post-Course Lifestyle Evaluations

The following lifestyle evaluations will give you a picture of your current strengths and weaknesses in four categories: perspective/motivation, fat management, nutrition, and fitness. Take your time in responding to the evaluations and base your answers on your attitudes or behavior. A special thanks to Danna Demetre for allowing us to use evaluations # 2, #3, & #4 taken from her book, Scale Down. To view her book and other resources go to www.dannademetre.com.

- Let's see if your attitudes or behavior has changed as a result of this class!
- Rate yourself on your first impression
- Don't go back and readjust your answers if you don't like your score
- Remember that this is a reality check. Just face the truth and move on!

Lifestyle Evaluation #1 – Perspective/Motivation

Please rate yourself (0 – Almost never; 1 – Sometimes; 2 – Often; 3 – Always)

_____ I see myself as a valued, unique individual.
_____ My choices and actions are morally responsible.
_____ I am thankful for the body given to me.
_____ My lifestyle habits are honorable to others and myself.
_____ I take responsibility for my body's size, shape and health.
_____ My attitude is this: I am not the center of the universe and I have a responsibility to help others.
_____ I understand that I have weaknesses and can overcome them with help.
_____ My personal goals are realistic and honorable.
_____ I take realistic steps toward my goals each day.
_____ I know that with consistent, healthy habits I can have a lean, healthy body.
_____ I am aware of the lies I believe about my body, looks, and health.
_____ I recognize and choose not to accept this negative thinking.
_____ I focus on the positive and strive to overcome obstacles in life.
_____ I am a work in progress and I benefit from each positive/healthy step I take.
_____ Everyday, I choose to make decisions that benefit my mind, body, attitude, health, family & Relationships.
_____ Everyday, I strive to resist temptations that threaten to chip away at my dreams and goals.

_____ Add the total of all scores.

Scoring
- 40-48 Excellent! You have a good perspective.
- 31-39 Good. Your perspective is usually working for you.
- 22-30 Fair. It's time to get a new focus…the truth!
- < 21   Alert! Alert! Change your perspective now!

Name _____

Lifestyle Evaluation #2 – Food Attitude Management

Please rate yourself (0 – Almost never; 1 – Sometimes; 2 – Often; 3 – Always)

_____ I feel in control of my food choices.

_____ I measure my size by how I look and feel, not the scale.

_____ I eat only when I'm hungry.

_____ I stop eating when I'm full.

_____ I understand why calories count.

_____ I eat four to five small meals or snacks per day.

_____ I limit my junk food, fast food, and desserts to less than 15% of my diet.

_____ I am happy with my body weight.

_____ I am happy with my size and shape.

_____ I can enjoy "fun food" without feeling guilty.

_____ I think about food only when I'm hungry.

_____ I can see myself eating and living in control.

_____ I walk or get purposeful exercise at least four times per week.

_____ I am very aware of my choices and how they affect my body.

_____ I say no to the latest diets or supplements promising quick results.

_____ I know if I'm going to be lean, I have to take daily action.

_____ Add the total of all scores.

Scoring

40-49 Excellent! You have a lean lifestyle.

31-40 Good. You're doing most things right!

22-31 Fair. It's time to take action.

< 21 Poor. Start with one step at a time

Name _____

Lifestyle Evaluation #3 – Nutrition

Please rate yourself (0 – Almost never; 1- Sometimes; 2 – Often; 3 – Always)

_____	I think about what I eat and how it impacts my health.
_____	I have high energy to do all the things I want and need to do.
_____	I read labels and choose many foods based on that information
_____	I eat two to three servings of fruit each day.
_____	I eat three to four servings of vegetables each day.
_____	I choose whole-grain products over more processed foods.
_____	I know how much fiber I'm eating daily.
_____	I drink ten to twelve glasses of water daily.
_____	I eat breakfast every day.
_____	I eat a good source of protein with my breakfast.
_____	I choose and eat lean protein with my lunch.
_____	I limit my empty calories to less than 15% of my total diet.
_____	I limit caffeine and other stimulants, such as over-the-counter diet aids, and energy drinks.
_____	I take a multivitamin supplement daily.
_____	I take an antioxidant supplement daily.
_____	I choose "healthy" fats in my diet such as flaxseed oil, fish oils, olive oil, or canola oil.
_____	Add the total of all scores.

Scoring

40-49   Excellent! Your body loves you!
31-40   Good. You're on the right track.
22-31   Fair. It's time to try a little more high-octane fuel.
<21   Poor. Your body is crying, "Help!"

Name _____

Lifestyle Evaluation #4 – Fitness

Please rate yourself (0 – Almost never; 1- Sometimes; 2 – Often; 3 – Always)

_____ I crave activity and find ways to move more each day.

_____ I enjoy exercise and how it makes my body feel.

_____ I have high energy to do all the things I want and need to do.

_____ I make exercise and activity a priority in my life.

_____ I understand the need for aerobic, strength, and flexibility training.

_____ I take the stairs or park far away whenever I can.

_____ I monitor my heart rate and know I am exercising safely.

_____ I am injury free and able to engage in most activities.

_____ Being healthy and fit is important to me.

_____ I listen to my body and know what it needs.

_____ I wear appropriate and quality shoes for exercise.

_____ I have a very active life and am moving throughout the day.

_____ I work out my major muscle groups two to three times each week.

_____ I can easily touch my toes without bending my knees.

_____ I maintain strong abdominal muscles.

_____ Add the total of all scores.

Scoring

40-49　Excellent! You're a fit machine!

31-40　Good. Stay consistent.

22-31　Fair. Use it or lose it!

< 21　 Poor. Take one small step and start moving!

Name _____

Lifestyle Evaluations Summary   Name _____

Have your attitudes or habits changed?

1. Look back at your score for the Lifestyle Evaluation #1 from the beginning of this 9-week grading period on page 85. What was your score from the original evaluation? _____
2. What was your score from the Lifestyle Evaluation this at the end of the quarter on page 115? _____
3. Has your perspective or motivation changed throughout the quarter?
4. What do you notice when you compare your answers from the original evaluation and the second one?

5. Look back at your score for the Lifestyle Evaluation #2 on Food Attitude Management on page 86. What was your original score? _____
6. What is your score on evaluation #2 at the end of the quarter on page 116? _____
7. Did you make improvements in this area?
8. How has this course affected your attitudes and habits in this area?

9. Look back at your score for the Lifestyle Evaluation #3 on Nutrition on page 87. What was your original score? _____
10. What is your score on evaluation #3 at the end of the quarter on page 117? _____
11. Are you making better nutritional choices than you were at the beginning of the semester?
12. List at least three positive changes you have made with regards to nutritional habits this semester?

13. Look back at your score for the Lifestyle Evaluation #4 on Fitness on page 88. What was your original score? _____
14. What is your score on evaluation #4 at the end of the quarter on page 118? _____
15. Have your attitudes about exercise or fitness changed this semester? Why or why not?

16. Do you understand the relationship between a healthy body and exercise?

17. What is one area of fitness that you have improved this semester?

Second Quarter

Journal Pages

Complete the following pages by recording your nutrition and exercise habits. Please complete questions as they appear on various pages.

Be honest about your habits and thoughts.

The purpose of the journal is to help you see a realistic picture of your habits (including your thoughts) and track the positive changes you make!

Every step takes you a little closer to your goal!

F.Y.I.

Some of the weekly journal pages look a little different this quarter. Instead of writing down everything you eat each day, you will just check off food groups that you have eaten. There are still a few weeks where you do record your food intake...just to help keep you on track! You will also check off if you are meeting your new goals (page   ) for exercise, nutrition, sleep, studying, etc. Remember to keep record of your exercise...especially for the Challenge! Good luck with your second quarter in this class...apply what you are learning and see how much better you will feel & look!

Second Quarter Week 1

Name_____

Think about what you ate each day. Check off the boxes that apply to your intake. Did you meet your food group requirements? Remember to fill in your exercise chart on the back of this page!

	Monday	Tuesday	Wednesday	Thursday	Friday	Saturday	Sunday
Water	☐☐☐☐ ☐☐☐☐	☐☐☐☐ ☐☐☐☐	☐☐☐☐ ☐☐☐☐	☐☐☐☐ ☐☐☐☐	☐☐☐☐ ☐☐☐☐	☐☐☐☐ ☐☐☐☐	☐☐☐☐ ☐☐☐☐
Grains	☐☐☐☐☐	☐☐☐☐☐	☐☐☐☐☐	☐☐☐☐☐	☐☐☐☐☐	☐☐☐☐☐	☐☐☐☐☐
Fruit	☐☐☐☐☐	☐☐☐☐☐	☐☐☐☐☐	☐☐☐☐☐	☐☐☐☐☐	☐☐☐☐☐	☐☐☐☐☐
Veggies	☐☐☐☐☐	☐☐☐☐☐	☐☐☐☐☐	☐☐☐☐☐	☐☐☐☐☐	☐☐☐☐☐	☐☐☐☐☐
Meat/Beans	☐☐☐☐	☐☐☐☐	☐☐☐☐	☐☐☐☐	☐☐☐☐	☐☐☐☐	☐☐☐☐
Dairy	☐☐☐☐	☐☐☐☐	☐☐☐☐	☐☐☐☐	☐☐☐☐	☐☐☐☐	☐☐☐☐
Coffee/Soft Drinks	☐☐☐☐	☐☐☐☐	☐☐☐☐	☐☐☐☐	☐☐☐☐	☐☐☐☐	☐☐☐☐
Discretionary Calories	☐☐☐☐☐	☐☐☐☐☐	☐☐☐☐☐	☐☐☐☐☐	☐☐☐☐☐	☐☐☐☐☐	☐☐☐☐☐
Vitamins	Yes ☐ No ☐	Yes ☐ No ☐	Yes ☐ No ☐	Yes ☐ No ☐	Yes ☐ No ☐	Yes ☐ No ☐	Yes ☐ No ☐
Minerals	Yes ☐ No ☐	Yes ☐ No ☐	Yes ☐ No ☐	Yes ☐ No ☐	Yes ☐ No ☐	Yes ☐ No ☐	Yes ☐ No ☐
Breakfast	Yes ☐ No ☐	Yes ☐ No ☐	Yes ☐ No ☐	Yes ☐ No ☐	Yes ☐ No ☐	Yes ☐ No ☐	Yes ☐ No ☐
Sleep	# hours ____	# hours ____	# hours ____	# hours ____	# hours ____	# hours ____	# hours ____
New daily nutrition goal...	Yes ☐ No ☐	Yes ☐ No ☐	Yes ☐ No ☐	Yes ☐ No ☐	Yes ☐ No ☐	Yes ☐ No ☐	Yes ☐ No ☐
New daily exercise goal...	Yes ☐ No ☐	Yes ☐ No ☐	Yes ☐ No ☐	Yes ☐ No ☐	Yes ☐ No ☐	Yes ☐ No ☐	Yes ☐ No ☐
Sleep goal...	Yes ☐ No ☐	Yes ☐ No ☐	Yes ☐ No ☐	Yes ☐ No ☐	Yes ☐ No ☐	Yes ☐ No ☐	Yes ☐ No ☐
Study goal...	Yes ☐ No ☐	Yes ☐ No ☐	Yes ☐ No ☐	Yes ☐ No ☐	Yes ☐ No ☐	Yes ☐ No ☐	Yes ☐ No ☐
Attitude goal...	Yes ☐ No ☐	Yes ☐ No ☐	Yes ☐ No ☐	Yes ☐ No ☐	Yes ☐ No ☐	Yes ☐ No ☐	Yes ☐ No ☐

© 2009 Betty Kern. Please don't make illegal copies of this page

How did you do this week with adding in new daily goals & strategies?"

Did it help you keep on track with your goals? Why or why not? Do you need to change something?

Second Quarter
Week #1

> "Mental will is a muscle that needs exercise, just like the muscles of the body."
> Lyn Jennings, 3-time World Cross Country Champ

Name_____

Strength Training Log

Exercises	Date	Date	Exercises	Date	Date
Chest			Arms		
Back			Core		
Shoulders			Legs/Glutes		

Cardio Log

	Cardio	#	Intensity	#
	Exercise	Mins	Level	Miles
Mon				
Tue				
Wed				
Thur				
Fri				
Sat				
Sun				
	Total		Total	
	Minutes	____	Miles	____

Nutrition Goal for this week:

Exercise Goal for this week:

© 2009 Betty Kern. Please don't make illegal copies of this page

	Monday	Tuesday	Wednesday	Thursday	Friday	Saturday	Sunday	Weekly Total
Ab Exercises								
Push-ups								

Week 2

Name_____

Think about what you ate each day. Check off the boxes that apply to your intake. Did you meet your food group requirements?
Remember to fill in your exercise chart on the back of this page!

	Monday	Tuesday	Wednesday	Thursday	Friday	Saturday	Sunday
Water	☐☐☐☐ ☐☐☐☐	☐☐☐☐ ☐☐☐☐	☐☐☐☐ ☐☐☐☐	☐☐☐☐ ☐☐☐☐	☐☐☐☐ ☐☐☐☐	☐☐☐☐ ☐☐☐☐	☐☐☐☐ ☐☐☐☐
Grains	☐☐☐☐☐☐	☐☐☐☐☐☐	☐☐☐☐☐☐	☐☐☐☐☐☐	☐☐☐☐☐☐	☐☐☐☐☐☐	☐☐☐☐☐☐
Fruit	☐☐☐☐☐☐	☐☐☐☐☐☐	☐☐☐☐☐☐	☐☐☐☐☐☐	☐☐☐☐☐☐	☐☐☐☐☐☐	☐☐☐☐☐☐
Veggies	☐☐☐☐☐☐	☐☐☐☐☐☐	☐☐☐☐☐☐	☐☐☐☐☐☐	☐☐☐☐☐☐	☐☐☐☐☐☐	☐☐☐☐☐☐
Meat/Beans	☐☐☐☐	☐☐☐☐	☐☐☐☐	☐☐☐☐	☐☐☐☐	☐☐☐☐	☐☐☐☐
Dairy	☐☐☐☐☐	☐☐☐☐☐	☐☐☐☐☐	☐☐☐☐☐	☐☐☐☐☐	☐☐☐☐☐	☐☐☐☐☐
Coffee/Soft Drinks	☐☐☐☐	☐☐☐☐	☐☐☐☐	☐☐☐☐	☐☐☐☐	☐☐☐☐	☐☐☐☐
Discretionary Calories	☐☐☐☐☐	☐☐☐☐☐	☐☐☐☐☐	☐☐☐☐☐	☐☐☐☐☐	☐☐☐☐☐	☐☐☐☐☐
Vitamins	Yes ☐ No ☐	Yes ☐ No ☐	Yes ☐ No ☐	Yes ☐ No ☐	Yes ☐ No ☐	Yes ☐ No ☐	Yes ☐ No ☐
Minerals	Yes ☐ No ☐	Yes ☐ No ☐	Yes ☐ No ☐	Yes ☐ No ☐	Yes ☐ No ☐	Yes ☐ No ☐	Yes ☐ No ☐
Breakfast	Yes ☐ No ☐	Yes ☐ No ☐	Yes ☐ No ☐	Yes ☐ No ☐	Yes ☐ No ☐	Yes ☐ No ☐	Yes ☐ No ☐
Sleep	# hours ____	# hours ____	# hours ____	# hours ____	# hours ____	# hours ____	# hours ____
New daily nutrition goal...	Yes ☐ No ☐	Yes ☐ No ☐	Yes ☐ No ☐	Yes ☐ No ☐	Yes ☐ No ☐	Yes ☐ No ☐	Yes ☐ No ☐
New daily exercise goal...	Yes ☐ No ☐	Yes ☐ No ☐	Yes ☐ No ☐	Yes ☐ No ☐	Yes ☐ No ☐	Yes ☐ No ☐	Yes ☐ No ☐
Sleep goal...	Yes ☐ No ☐	Yes ☐ No ☐	Yes ☐ No ☐	Yes ☐ No ☐	Yes ☐ No ☐	Yes ☐ No ☐	Yes ☐ No ☐
Study goal...	Yes ☐ No ☐	Yes ☐ No ☐	Yes ☐ No ☐	Yes ☐ No ☐	Yes ☐ No ☐	Yes ☐ No ☐	Yes ☐ No ☐
Attitude goal...	Yes ☐ No ☐	Yes ☐ No ☐	Yes ☐ No ☐	Yes ☐ No ☐	Yes ☐ No ☐	Yes ☐ No ☐	Yes ☐ No ☐

© 2009 Betty Kern. Please don't make illegal copies of this page

How did your new habits go this week?

Are you making progress? Why or why not?

Week #2

> "There lies within all of us an athlete just waiting to be discovered."
> George Sheahan

Name_____

Strength Training Log

Exercises	Date	Date	Exercises	Date	Date
			Arms		
Chest					
Back			Core		
Shoulders			Legs/Glutes		

Cardio Log

	Cardio	#	Intensity	#
	Exercise	Mins	Level	Miles
Mon				
Tue				
Wed				
Thur				
Fri				
Sat				
Sun				
	Total Minutes	____	Total Miles	____

Nutrition Goal for this week:

_____

Exercise Goal for this week:

© 2009 Betty Kern. Please don't make illegal copies of this page

	Monday	Tuesday	Wednesday	Thursday	Friday	Saturday	Sunday	Weekly Total	Challenge Totals
Ab Exercises									
Push-ups									

Week 3

Monday water ☐☐☐☐☐☐☐☐

Breakfast: _____ dairy   ☐☐☐☐☐☐
_____ veggies ☐☐☐☐☐☐
Lunch: _____ fruit   ☐☐☐☐☐☐
_____ protein ☐☐☐☐
Snack: _____ carbs   ☐☐☐☐☐☐
Dinner: _____ healthy fats ☐☐☐☐
_____ soft drinks ____ coffee__
_____ Sleep # hours _____
Snack: _____ Vitamins Yes ☐   No ☐

Discretionary Calories:
Fast food ☐☐☐☐☐   Sweets ☐☐☐☐☐
Junk food ☐☐☐☐☐   Other ☐☐☐☐☐

Tuesday water ☐☐☐☐☐☐☐☐

Breakfast: _____ dairy   ☐☐☐☐☐☐
_____ veggies ☐☐☐☐☐☐
Lunch: _____ fruit   ☐☐☐☐☐☐
_____ protein ☐☐☐☐
Snack: _____ carbs   ☐☐☐☐☐☐
Dinner: _____ healthy fats ☐☐☐☐
_____ soft drinks ___coffee__
_____ Sleep # hours _____
Snack: _____ Vitamins Yes ☐   No ☐

Discretionary Calories:
Fast food ☐☐☐☐☐   Sweets ☐☐☐☐☐
Junk food ☐☐☐☐☐   Other ☐☐☐☐☐

Five Ways to Boost Your Metabolism
Fitness Magazine, November 2007

1. *Eat breakfast.*
2. *Lift weights! A pound of muscle burns twice as many calories than fat!*
3. *Add some lean protein to your diet...chicken, fish, eggs, or nuts.*
4. *Eat smaller meals more often.*
5. *Mix up your aerobic exercise!*

Wednesday water ☐☐☐☐☐☐☐☐

Breakfast: _____ dairy   ☐☐☐☐☐☐
_____ veggies ☐☐☐☐☐☐
Lunch: _____ fruit   ☐☐☐☐☐☐
_____ protein ☐☐☐☐
Snack: _____ carbs   ☐☐☐☐☐☐
Dinner: _____ healthy fats ☐☐☐☐
_____ soft drinks ____ coffee__
_____ Sleep # hours _____
Snack: _____ Vitamins Yes ☐   No ☐

Discretionary Calories:
Fast food ☐☐☐☐☐   Sweets ☐☐☐☐☐
Junk food ☐☐☐☐☐   Other ☐☐☐☐☐

Thursday water ☐☐☐☐☐☐☐☐

Breakfast: _____ dairy   ☐☐☐☐☐☐
_____ veggies ☐☐☐☐☐☐
Lunch: _____ fruit   ☐☐☐☐☐☐
_____ protein ☐☐☐☐
Snack: _____ carbs   ☐☐☐☐☐☐
Dinner: _____ healthy fats ☐☐☐☐
_____ soft drinks ____ coffee__
_____ Sleep # hours _____
Snack: _____ Vitamins Yes ☐   No ☐

Discretionary Calories:
Fast food ☐☐☐☐☐   Sweets ☐☐☐☐☐
Junk food ☐☐☐☐☐   Other ☐☐☐☐☐

Friday water ☐☐☐☐☐☐☐☐

Breakfast: _____ dairy   ☐☐☐☐☐☐
_____ veggies ☐☐☐☐☐☐
Lunch: _____ fruit   ☐☐☐☐☐☐
_____ protein ☐☐☐☐
Snack: _____ carbs   ☐☐☐☐☐☐
Dinner: _____ healthy fats ☐☐☐☐
_____ soft drinks ____ coffee__
_____ Sleep # hours _____
Snack: _____ Vitamins Yes ☐   No ☐

Discretionary Calories:
Fast food ☐☐☐☐☐   Sweets ☐☐☐☐☐
Junk food ☐☐☐☐☐   Other ☐☐☐☐☐

"Commit yourself to constant self-improvement. The joy is truly in the journey!"
Denise Austin

Saturday water ☐☐☐☐☐☐☐☐

Breakfast: _____ dairy   ☐☐☐☐☐☐
_____ veggies ☐☐☐☐☐☐
Lunch: _____ fruit   ☐☐☐☐☐☐
_____ protein ☐☐☐☐
Snack: _____ carbs   ☐☐☐☐☐☐
Dinner: _____ healthy fats ☐☐☐☐
_____ soft drinks ____ coffee__
_____ Sleep # hours _____
Snack: _____ Vitamins Yes ☐   No ☐

Discretionary Calories:
Fast food ☐☐☐☐☐   Sweets ☐☐☐☐☐
Junk food ☐☐☐☐☐   Other ☐☐☐☐☐

Sunday water ☐☐☐☐☐☐☐☐

Breakfast: _____ dairy   ☐☐☐☐☐☐
_____ veggies ☐☐☐☐☐☐
Lunch: _____ fruit   ☐☐☐☐☐☐
_____ protein ☐☐☐☐
Snack: _____ carbs   ☐☐☐☐☐☐
Dinner: _____ healthy fats ☐☐☐☐
_____ soft drinks ____ coffee__
_____ Sleep # hours _____
Snack: _____ Vitamins Yes ☐   No ☐

Discretionary Calories:
Fast food ☐☐☐☐☐   Sweets ☐☐☐☐☐
Junk food ☐☐☐☐☐   Other ☐☐☐☐☐

How are your workouts going?

Are you getting in some exercise on the weekend?

Find a friend or family member to workout with...it will be more fun and he/she will help you make it a habit!

Week #3

> "Change your thoughts and you will change your world."
> Norman Vincent Peale

Name_____

Strength Training Log

Exercises	Date	Date	Exercises	Date	Date
Chest			Arms		
Back			Core		
Shoulders			Legs/Glutes		

Cardio Log

	Cardio Exercise	# Mins	Intensity Level	# Miles
Mon				
Tue				
Wed				
Thur				
Fri				
Sat				
Sun				
	Total Minutes	____	Total Miles	____

Nutrition Goal for this week:

_____

Exercise Goal for this week:

© 2009 Betty Kern. Please don't make illegal copies of this page

	Monday	Tuesday	Wednesday	Thursday	Friday	Saturday	Sunday	Weekly Total	Challenge Total
Ab Exercises									
Push-ups									

128

Week 4

Name_____

Think about what you ate each day. Check off the boxes that apply to your intake. Did you meet your food group requirements? Remember to fill in your exercise chart on the back of this page!

	Monday	Tuesday	Wednesday	Thursday	Friday	Saturday	Sunday
Water	☐☐☐☐ ☐☐☐☐	☐☐☐☐ ☐☐☐☐	☐☐☐☐ ☐☐☐☐	☐☐☐☐ ☐☐☐☐	☐☐☐☐ ☐☐☐☐	☐☐☐☐ ☐☐☐☐	☐☐☐☐ ☐☐☐☐
Grains	☐☐☐☐☐☐	☐☐☐☐☐☐	☐☐☐☐☐☐	☐☐☐☐☐☐	☐☐☐☐☐☐	☐☐☐☐☐☐	☐☐☐☐☐☐
Fruit	☐☐☐☐☐☐	☐☐☐☐☐☐	☐☐☐☐☐☐	☐☐☐☐☐☐	☐☐☐☐☐☐	☐☐☐☐☐☐	☐☐☐☐☐☐
Veggies	☐☐☐☐☐☐	☐☐☐☐☐☐	☐☐☐☐☐☐	☐☐☐☐☐☐	☐☐☐☐☐☐	☐☐☐☐☐☐	☐☐☐☐☐☐
Meat/Beans	☐☐☐☐	☐☐☐☐	☐☐☐☐	☐☐☐☐	☐☐☐☐	☐☐☐☐	☐☐☐☐
Dairy	☐☐☐☐☐	☐☐☐☐☐	☐☐☐☐☐	☐☐☐☐☐	☐☐☐☐☐	☐☐☐☐☐	☐☐☐☐☐
Coffee/Soft Drinks	☐☐☐☐	☐☐☐☐	☐☐☐☐	☐☐☐☐	☐☐☐☐	☐☐☐☐	☐☐☐☐
Discretionary Calories	☐☐☐☐☐	☐☐☐☐☐	☐☐☐☐☐	☐☐☐☐☐	☐☐☐☐☐	☐☐☐☐☐	☐☐☐☐☐
Vitamins	Yes ☐ No ☐	Yes ☐ No ☐	Yes ☐ No ☐	Yes ☐ No ☐	Yes ☐ No ☐	Yes ☐ No ☐	Yes ☐ No ☐
Minerals	Yes ☐ No ☐	Yes ☐ No ☐	Yes ☐ No ☐	Yes ☐ No ☐	Yes ☐ No ☐	Yes ☐ No ☐	Yes ☐ No ☐
Breakfast	Yes ☐ No ☐	Yes ☐ No ☐	Yes ☐ No ☐	Yes ☐ No ☐	Yes ☐ No ☐	Yes ☐ No ☐	Yes ☐ No ☐
Sleep	# hours ____	# hours ____	# hours ____	# hours ____	# hours ____	# hours ____	# hours ____
New daily nutrition goal...	Yes ☐ No ☐	Yes ☐ No ☐	Yes ☐ No ☐	Yes ☐ No ☐	Yes ☐ No ☐	Yes ☐ No ☐	Yes ☐ No ☐
New daily exercise goal...	Yes ☐ No ☐	Yes ☐ No ☐	Yes ☐ No ☐	Yes ☐ No ☐	Yes ☐ No ☐	Yes ☐ No ☐	Yes ☐ No ☐
Sleep goal...	Yes ☐ No ☐	Yes ☐ No ☐	Yes ☐ No ☐	Yes ☐ No ☐	Yes ☐ No ☐	Yes ☐ No ☐	Yes ☐ No ☐
Study goal...	Yes ☐ No ☐	Yes ☐ No ☐	Yes ☐ No ☐	Yes ☐ No ☐	Yes ☐ No ☐	Yes ☐ No ☐	Yes ☐ No ☐
Attitude goal...	Yes ☐ No ☐	Yes ☐ No ☐	Yes ☐ No ☐	Yes ☐ No ☐	Yes ☐ No ☐	Yes ☐ No ☐	Yes ☐ No ☐

© 2009 Betty Kern. Please don't make illegal copies of this page

Has eating healthier and exercising regularly affected your self-esteem, body-image or self-confidence?

Week #4

"What would it be like if we had no courage to attempt anything new?"
Vincent Van Gogh

Name_____

Strength Training Log

Exercises	Date	Date	Exercises	Date	Date
Chest			Arms		
Back			Core		
Shoulders			Legs/Glutes		

Cardio Log

Cardio	#	Intensity	#
Exercise	Mins	Level	Miles
Mon			
Tue			
Wed			
Thur			
Fri			
Sat			
Sun			
Total		Total	
Minutes	____	Miles	____

Nutrition Goal for this week:

_____

Exercise Goal for this week:

© 2009 Betty Kern. Please don't make illegal copies of this page

	Monday	Tuesday	Wednesday	Thursday	Friday	Saturday	Sunday	Weekly Total	Challenge Total
Ab Exercises									
Push-ups									

My Pyramid Tracker Assignment

Return to the web site www.MyPyramid.gov.
Go to the section **My Pyramid Tracker**.
Enter in 24 hours worth of physical activity and eating habits.

1. Click on **"Assess Your Food Intake."**
   Enter the foods you have eaten in a 24-hour period including the amount you ate.
   Analyze the intake under **"My Pyramid Recommendations"** and **print** out the results.
   Next click on the **"Nutrient Intake"** at the bottom of the page and **print** out the results.

2. Go to the **"Physical Activity"** section and click on **"Standard Option."**
   Calculate your physical activity score by entering in any physical activity for the last 24 hours.
   Click on **"Physical Activity Analysis"** and determine your physical activity score.
   Print out the page with your **"Physical Activity Score."**

3. At the top of the Physical Activity page, select **"Energy Balance Analysis."**
   Calculate your **"Energy Balance"** and **print** out the results.

   You should have four pages to turn in for this assignment.
   Make sure your name is on all four pages and staple them together.

4. *On the back of the last page, answer the following:*
   How are you doing with your nutrition and exercise habits?
   Are you meeting the pyramid recommendations?
   In what areas of nutrition are you doing well?
   What areas of your diet do you need to improve? (give specifics)
   Are you meeting the recommendations for physical activity?
   How could you improve your physical activity habits?

132

Week 5

Monday water ☐☐☐☐☐☐☐☐☐
Breakfast: _____ dairy ☐☐☐☐☐☐
_____ veggies ☐☐☐☐☐☐
Lunch: _____ fruit ☐☐☐☐☐☐
_____ protein ☐☐☐☐
Snack: _____ carbs ☐☐☐☐☐☐
Dinner: _____ healthy fats ☐☐☐☐☐
_____ soft drinks ___ coffee __
_____ Sleep # hours _____
Snack: _____ Vitamins Yes ☐ No ☐

Discretionary Calories:
Fast food ☐☐☐☐ Sweets ☐☐☐☐☐
Junk food ☐☐☐☐☐ Other ☐☐☐☐☐

Tuesday water ☐☐☐☐☐☐☐☐☐
Breakfast: _____ dairy ☐☐☐☐☐☐
_____ veggies ☐☐☐☐☐☐
Lunch: _____ fruit ☐☐☐☐☐☐
_____ protein ☐☐☐☐
Snack: _____ carbs ☐☐☐☐☐☐
Dinner: _____ healthy fats ☐☐☐☐☐
_____ soft drinks __ coffee __
_____ Sleep # hours _____
Snack: _____ Vitamins Yes ☐ No ☐

Discretionary Calories:
Fast food ☐☐☐☐ Sweets ☐☐☐☐☐
Junk food ☐☐☐☐☐ Other ☐☐☐☐☐

Keep striving to eat the correct number of servings of the food groups daily!

Watch out for those empty calories that don't provide any nutritional value...usually in drinks and sweets! When a holiday or special occasion approaches, go in with a plan!
Enjoy some of the goodies...just don't overindulge!

Remember to get enough water and sleep!
It will help you look and feel your best!

Wednesday water ☐☐☐☐☐☐☐☐☐
Breakfast: _____ dairy ☐☐☐☐☐
_____ veggies ☐☐☐☐
Lunch: _____ fruit ☐☐☐☐☐
_____ protein ☐☐☐☐
Snack: _____ carbs ☐☐☐☐☐
Dinner: _____ healthy fats ☐☐☐☐
_____ soft drinks ___ coffee __
_____ Sleep # hours _____
Snack: _____ Vitamins Yes ☐ No ☐

Discretionary Calories:
Fast food ☐☐☐☐ Sweets ☐☐☐☐☐
Junk food ☐☐☐☐☐ Other ☐☐☐☐☐

Thursday water ☐☐☐☐☐☐☐☐☐
Breakfast: _____ dairy ☐☐☐☐☐
_____ veggies ☐☐☐☐
Lunch: _____ fruit ☐☐☐☐☐
_____ protein ☐☐☐☐
Snack: _____ carbs ☐☐☐☐☐
Dinner: _____ healthy fats ☐☐☐☐
_____ soft drinks ___ coffee __
_____ Sleep # hours _____
Snack: _____ Vitamins Yes ☐ No ☐

Discretionary Calories:
Fast food ☐☐☐☐ Sweets ☐☐☐☐☐
Junk food ☐☐☐☐☐ Other ☐☐☐☐☐

Friday water ☐☐☐☐☐☐☐☐☐
Breakfast: _____ dairy ☐☐☐☐☐
_____ veggies ☐☐☐☐
Lunch: _____ fruit ☐☐☐☐☐
_____ protein ☐☐☐☐
Snack: _____ carbs ☐☐☐☐☐
Dinner: _____ healthy fats ☐☐☐☐
_____ soft drinks ___ coffee __
_____ Sleep # hours _____
Snack: _____ Vitamins Yes ☐ No ☐

Discretionary Calories:
Fast food ☐☐☐☐ Sweets ☐☐☐☐☐
Junk food ☐☐☐☐☐ Other ☐☐☐☐☐

Fear less, hope more, eat less, chew more, whine less, breathe more, talk less, say more, love more and all good things will be yours. Swedish Proverb

Saturday water ☐☐☐☐☐☐☐☐☐
Breakfast: _____ dairy ☐☐☐☐☐
_____ veggies ☐☐☐☐☐
Lunch: _____ fruit ☐☐☐☐☐☐
_____ protein ☐☐☐☐
Snack: _____ carbs ☐☐☐☐☐☐
Dinner: _____ healthy fats ☐☐☐☐
_____ soft drinks ___ coffee __
_____ Sleep # hours _____
Snack: _____ Vitamins Yes ☐ No ☐

Discretionary Calories:
Fast food ☐☐☐☐ Sweets ☐☐☐☐☐
Junk food ☐☐☐☐☐ Other ☐☐☐☐☐

Sunday water ☐☐☐☐☐☐☐☐☐
Breakfast: _____ dairy ☐☐☐☐☐
_____ veggies ☐☐☐☐☐
Lunch: _____ fruit ☐☐☐☐☐☐
_____ protein ☐☐☐☐
Snack: _____ carbs ☐☐☐☐☐☐
Dinner: _____ healthy fats ☐☐☐☐
_____ soft drinks ___ coffee __
_____ Sleep # hours _____
Snack: _____ Vitamins Yes ☐ No ☐

Discretionary Calories:
Fast food ☐☐☐☐ Sweets ☐☐☐☐☐
Junk food ☐☐☐☐☐ Other ☐☐☐☐☐

Exercise will improve your self-image!
Really, it will!

You will feel more in control of your body and the choices you make concerning nutrition and fitness! You will walk with confidence and people will notice!

Choose to ignore the false advertisements and lies around you...become the person you were meant to be!

Week #5

"One thing is clear from hundreds of studies of weight control conducted over the last 20 years without regular physical activity weight control usually cannot be achieved."
                                                                 Tim Byers

Name_____

Strength Training Log   ## Cardio Log

Exercises	Date	Date	Exercises	Date	Date
Chest			Arms		
Back			Core		
Shoulders			Legs/Glutes		

	Cardio	#	Intensity	#
	Exercise	Mins	Level	Miles
Mon				
Tue				
Wed				
Thur				
Fri				
Sat				
Sun				
	Total		Total	
	Minutes	____	Miles	____

Nutrition Goal for this week:

_____

Exercise Goal for this week:

© 2009 Betty Kern. Please don't make illegal copies of this page

	Monday	Tuesday	Wednesday	Thursday	Friday	Saturday	Sunday	Weekly Total	Challenge Total
Ab Exercises									
Push-ups									

Week 6

Name_____

Think about what you ate each day. Check off the boxes that apply to your intake. Did you meet your food group requirements? Remember to fill in your exercise chart on the back of this page!

	Monday	Tuesday	Wednesday	Thursday	Friday	Saturday	Sunday
Water	☐☐☐☐ ☐☐☐☐	☐☐☐☐ ☐☐☐☐	☐☐☐☐ ☐☐☐☐	☐☐☐☐ ☐☐☐☐	☐☐☐☐ ☐☐☐☐	☐☐☐☐ ☐☐☐☐	☐☐☐☐ ☐☐☐☐
Grains	☐☐☐☐☐	☐☐☐☐☐	☐☐☐☐☐	☐☐☐☐☐	☐☐☐☐☐	☐☐☐☐☐	☐☐☐☐☐
Fruit	☐☐☐☐☐	☐☐☐☐☐	☐☐☐☐☐	☐☐☐☐☐	☐☐☐☐☐	☐☐☐☐☐	☐☐☐☐☐
Veggies	☐☐☐☐☐	☐☐☐☐☐	☐☐☐☐☐	☐☐☐☐☐	☐☐☐☐☐	☐☐☐☐☐	☐☐☐☐☐
Meat/Beans	☐☐☐☐	☐☐☐☐	☐☐☐☐	☐☐☐☐	☐☐☐☐	☐☐☐☐	☐☐☐☐
Dairy	☐☐☐☐☐	☐☐☐☐☐	☐☐☐☐☐	☐☐☐☐☐	☐☐☐☐☐	☐☐☐☐☐	☐☐☐☐☐
Coffee/Soft Drinks	☐☐☐☐	☐☐☐☐	☐☐☐☐	☐☐☐☐	☐☐☐☐	☐☐☐☐	☐☐☐☐
Discretionary Calories	☐☐☐☐☐	☐☐☐☐☐	☐☐☐☐☐	☐☐☐☐☐	☐☐☐☐☐	☐☐☐☐☐	☐☐☐☐☐
Vitamins	Yes ☐ No ☐	Yes ☐ No ☐	Yes ☐ No ☐	Yes ☐ No ☐	Yes ☐ No ☐	Yes ☐ No ☐	Yes ☐ No ☐
Minerals	Yes ☐ No ☐	Yes ☐ No ☐	Yes ☐ No ☐	Yes ☐ No ☐	Yes ☐ No ☐	Yes ☐ No ☐	Yes ☐ No ☐
Breakfast	Yes ☐ No ☐	Yes ☐ No ☐	Yes ☐ No ☐	Yes ☐ No ☐	Yes ☐ No ☐	Yes ☐ No ☐	Yes ☐ No ☐
Sleep	# hours ____	# hours ____	# hours ____	# hours ____	# hours ____	# hours ____	# hours ____
Nutrition goal...	Yes ☐ No ☐	Yes ☐ No ☐	Yes ☐ No ☐	Yes ☐ No ☐	Yes ☐ No ☐	Yes ☐ No ☐	Yes ☐ No ☐
Exercise goal...	Yes ☐ No ☐	Yes ☐ No ☐	Yes ☐ No ☐	Yes ☐ No ☐	Yes ☐ No ☐	Yes ☐ No ☐	Yes ☐ No ☐
Sleep goal...	Yes ☐ No ☐	Yes ☐ No ☐	Yes ☐ No ☐	Yes ☐ No ☐	Yes ☐ No ☐	Yes ☐ No ☐	Yes ☐ No ☐
Study goal...	Yes ☐ No ☐	Yes ☐ No ☐	Yes ☐ No ☐	Yes ☐ No ☐	Yes ☐ No ☐	Yes ☐ No ☐	Yes ☐ No ☐
Attitude goal...	Yes ☐ No ☐	Yes ☐ No ☐	Yes ☐ No ☐	Yes ☐ No ☐	Yes ☐ No ☐	Yes ☐ No ☐	Yes ☐ No ☐

© 2009 Betty Kern. Please don't make illegal copies of this page

How are you feeling? Do you have more energy? Have your healthy habits made an impact on your life? How?

Week #6

"Attitude is everything! Keep a positive attitude and you will be surprised how much you can do both physically and mentally!"
Betty Kern

Name_____

Strength Training Log

Cardio Log

Exercises	Date	Date	Exercises	Date	Date
Chest			Arms		
Back			Core		
Shoulders			Legs/Glutes		

	Cardio	#	Intensity	#
	Exercise	Mins	Level	Miles
Mon				
Tue				
Wed				
Thur				
Fri				
Sat				
Sun				
	Total		Total	
	Minutes	____	Miles	____

Nutrition Goal for this week:

_____

Exercise Goal for this week:

© 2009 Betty Kern. Please don't make illegal copies of this page

	Monday	Tuesday	Wednesday	Thursday	Friday	Saturday	Sunday	Weekly Total	Challenge Total
Ab Exercises									
Push-ups									

Week 7

Monday water ☐☐☐☐☐☐☐☐☐
Breakfast: _____ dairy ☐☐☐☐☐☐
_____ veggies ☐☐☐☐☐☐
Lunch: _____ fruit ☐☐☐☐☐☐
_____ protein ☐☐☐☐
Snack: _____ carbs ☐☐☐☐☐☐
Dinner: _____ healthy fats ☐☐☐☐☐
_____ soft drinks ___ coffee__
_____ Sleep # hours _____
Snack: _____ Vitamins Yes ☐ No ☐

Discretionary Calories:
   Fast food ☐☐☐☐☐   Sweets ☐☐☐☐☐
   Junk food ☐☐☐☐☐   Other ☐☐☐☐☐

Tuesday water ☐☐☐☐☐☐☐☐☐
Breakfast: _____ dairy ☐☐☐☐☐☐
_____ veggies ☐☐☐☐☐☐
Lunch: _____ fruit ☐☐☐☐☐☐
_____ protein ☐☐☐☐
Snack: _____ carbs ☐☐☐☐☐☐
Dinner: _____ healthy fats ☐☐☐☐☐
_____ soft drinks ___ coffee__
_____ Sleep # hours _____
Snack: _____ Vitamins Yes ☐ No ☐

Discretionary Calories:
   Fast food ☐☐☐☐☐   Sweets ☐☐☐☐☐
   Junk food ☐☐☐☐☐   Other ☐☐☐☐☐

You can change your workouts to continue to challenge your body by manipulating these components of fitness…(page 34)

F. _____
I. _____
T. _____
T. _____
E. _____
E. _____

There is no excuse for boredom…change things around…try new activities…have fun!

Wednesday water ☐☐☐☐☐☐☐☐☐
Breakfast: _____ dairy ☐☐☐☐☐☐
_____ veggies ☐☐☐☐
Lunch: _____ fruit ☐☐☐☐☐
_____ protein ☐☐☐☐
Snack: _____ carbs ☐☐☐☐☐
Dinner: _____ healthy fats ☐☐☐☐
_____ soft drinks ___ coffee__
_____ Sleep # hours _____
Snack: _____ Vitamins Yes ☐ No ☐

Discretionary Calories:
   Fast food ☐☐☐☐☐   Sweets ☐☐☐☐☐
   Junk food ☐☐☐☐☐   Other ☐☐☐☐☐

Thursday water ☐☐☐☐☐☐☐☐☐
Breakfast: _____ dairy ☐☐☐☐☐☐
_____ veggies ☐☐☐☐
Lunch: _____ fruit ☐☐☐☐☐
_____ protein ☐☐☐☐
Snack: _____ carbs ☐☐☐☐☐
Dinner: _____ healthy fats ☐☐☐☐
_____ soft drinks ___ coffee__
_____ Sleep # hours _____
Snack: _____ Vitamins Yes ☐ No ☐

Discretionary Calories:
   Fast food ☐☐☐☐☐   Sweets ☐☐☐☐☐
   Junk food ☐☐☐☐☐   Other ☐☐☐☐☐

Friday water ☐☐☐☐☐☐☐☐☐
Breakfast: _____ dairy ☐☐☐☐☐☐
_____ veggies ☐☐☐☐
Lunch: _____ fruit ☐☐☐☐☐
_____ protein ☐☐☐☐
Snack: _____ carbs ☐☐☐☐☐
Dinner: _____ healthy fats ☐☐☐☐
_____ soft drinks ___ coffee__
_____ Sleep # hours _____
Snack: _____ Vitamins Yes ☐ No ☐

Discretionary Calories:
   Fast food ☐☐☐☐☐   Sweets ☐☐☐☐☐
   Junk food ☐☐☐☐☐   Other ☐☐☐☐☐

Happiness is a butterfly, which, when pursued, is always just beyond your grasp, but which, if you sit down quietly, may alight upon you. Nathaniel Hawthorne

Saturday water ☐☐☐☐☐☐☐☐☐
Breakfast: _____ dairy ☐☐☐☐☐
_____ veggies ☐☐☐☐☐
Lunch: _____ fruit ☐☐☐☐☐☐
_____ protein ☐☐☐☐
Snack: _____ carbs ☐☐☐☐☐☐
Dinner: _____ healthy fats ☐☐☐☐
_____ soft drinks ___ coffee__
_____ Sleep # hours _____
Snack: _____ Vitamins Yes ☐ No ☐

Discretionary Calories:
   Fast food ☐☐☐☐☐   Sweets ☐☐☐☐☐
   Junk food ☐☐☐☐☐   Other ☐☐☐☐☐

Sunday water ☐☐☐☐☐☐☐☐☐
Breakfast: _____ dairy ☐☐☐☐☐☐
_____ veggies ☐☐☐☐☐☐
Lunch: _____ fruit ☐☐☐☐☐☐
_____ protein ☐☐☐☐☐
Snack: _____ carbs ☐☐☐☐☐☐
Dinner: _____ healthy fats ☐☐☐☐
_____ soft drinks ___ coffee__
_____ Sleep # hours _____
Snack: _____ Vitamins Yes ☐ No ☐

Discretionary Calories:
   Fast food ☐☐☐☐☐   Sweets ☐☐☐☐☐
   Junk food ☐☐☐☐☐   Other ☐☐☐☐☐

What kind of "things" are you thinking about?
Are you filling your mind with messages that will bring you down or lift you up?
Are your thoughts filled with 'I can" or 'I can't'…
I am not good enough…thin enough…smart enough…gifted enough…good looking enough…to do ….
If so, change your messages around…tell yourself that you can do anything you set your mind to accomplishing! Your thoughts will become a self-fulfilling prophecy!

Week #7

"Life rewards action!"
Jay McGraw

Name_____

Strength Training Log | Cardio Log

Exercises	Date	Date	Exercises	Date	Date
Chest			Arms		
Back			Core		
Shoulders			Legs/Glutes		

	Cardio	#	Intensity	#
	Exercise	Mins	Level	Miles
Mon				
Tue				
Wed				
Thur				
Fri				
Sat				
Sun				
	Total		Total	
	Minutes	____	Miles	____

Nutrition Goal for this week:

_____

Exercise Goal for this week:

© 2009 Betty Kern. Please don't make illegal copies of this page

	Monday	Tuesday	Wednesday	Thursday	Friday	Saturday	Sunday	Weekly Total	Challenge Total
Ab Exercises									
Push-ups									

Week 8

Monday water ☐☐☐☐☐☐☐☐
Breakfast: _____ dairy ☐☐☐☐☐
_____ veggies ☐☐☐☐☐
Lunch: _____ fruit ☐☐☐☐
_____ protein ☐☐☐☐
Snack: _____ carbs ☐☐☐☐☐
Dinner: _____ healthy fats ☐☐☐☐
_____ soft drinks ___ coffee___
_____ Sleep # hours _____
Snack: _____ Vitamins Yes ☐ No ☐

Discretionary Calories:
Fast food ☐☐☐☐☐ Sweets ☐☐☐☐☐
Junk food ☐☐☐☐☐ Other ☐☐☐☐☐

Tuesday water ☐☐☐☐☐☐☐☐
Breakfast: _____ dairy ☐☐☐☐☐
_____ veggies ☐☐☐☐☐
Lunch: _____ fruit ☐☐☐☐
_____ protein ☐☐☐☐
Snack: _____ carbs ☐☐☐☐☐
Dinner: _____ healthy fats ☐☐☐☐
_____ soft drinks ___ coffee___
_____ Sleep # hours _____
Snack: _____ Vitamins Yes ☐ No ☐

Discretionary Calories:
Fast food ☐☐☐☐☐ Sweets ☐☐☐☐☐
Junk food ☐☐☐☐☐ Other ☐☐☐☐☐

Strength training is one of the most effective ways to truly change the 'shape' of your body. If you haven't worked out with weights before, this will take some time...be patient and consistent!
The results will be worth it!
You can lift free weights, use machines, exercise bands, or perform calisthenics to strength train. It doesn't matter which type of strength training exercise you do, just do it!
You will add muscle, shape and tone your muscles, boost your metabolism, look and feel great!

Wednesday water ☐☐☐☐☐☐☐☐
Breakfast: _____ dairy ☐☐☐☐☐
_____ veggies ☐☐☐☐☐
Lunch: _____ fruit ☐☐☐☐
_____ protein ☐☐☐☐
Snack: _____ carbs ☐☐☐☐☐
Dinner: _____ healthy fats ☐☐☐☐
_____ soft drinks ___ coffee___
_____ Sleep # hours _____
Snack: _____ Vitamins Yes ☐ No ☐

Discretionary Calories:
Fast food ☐☐☐☐☐ Sweets ☐☐☐☐☐
Junk food ☐☐☐☐☐ Other ☐☐☐☐☐

Thursday water ☐☐☐☐☐☐☐☐
Breakfast: _____ dairy ☐☐☐☐☐
_____ veggies ☐☐☐☐☐
Lunch: _____ fruit ☐☐☐☐
_____ protein ☐☐☐☐
Snack: _____ carbs ☐☐☐☐☐
Dinner: _____ healthy fats ☐☐☐☐
_____ soft drinks ___ coffee___
_____ Sleep # hours _____
Snack: _____ Vitamins Yes ☐ No ☐

Discretionary Calories:
Fast food ☐☐☐☐☐ Sweets ☐☐☐☐☐
Junk food ☐☐☐☐☐ Other ☐☐☐☐☐

Friday water ☐☐☐☐☐☐☐☐
Breakfast: _____ dairy ☐☐☐☐☐
_____ veggies ☐☐☐☐☐
Lunch: _____ fruit ☐☐☐☐
_____ protein ☐☐☐☐
Snack: _____ carbs ☐☐☐☐☐
Dinner: _____ healthy fats ☐☐☐☐
_____ soft drinks ___ coffee___
_____ Sleep # hours _____
Snack: _____ Vitamins Yes ☐ No ☐

Discretionary Calories:
Fast food ☐☐☐☐☐ Sweets ☐☐☐☐☐
Junk food ☐☐☐☐☐ Other ☐☐☐☐☐

"The greatest success is successful self-acceptance."
Ben Sweet

Saturday water ☐☐☐☐☐☐☐☐
Breakfast: _____ dairy ☐☐☐☐☐
_____ veggies ☐☐☐☐☐
Lunch: _____ fruit ☐☐☐☐
_____ protein ☐☐☐☐
Snack: _____ carbs ☐☐☐☐☐
Dinner: _____ healthy fats ☐☐☐☐
_____ soft drinks ___ coffee___
_____ Sleep # hours _____
Snack: _____ Vitamins Yes ☐ No ☐

Discretionary Calories:
Fast food ☐☐☐☐☐ Sweets ☐☐☐☐☐
Junk food ☐☐☐☐☐ Other ☐☐☐☐☐

Sunday water ☐☐☐☐☐☐☐☐
Breakfast: _____ dairy ☐☐☐☐☐
_____ veggies ☐☐☐☐☐
Lunch: _____ fruit ☐☐☐☐
_____ protein ☐☐☐☐
Snack: _____ carbs ☐☐☐☐☐
Dinner: _____ healthy fats ☐☐☐☐
_____ soft drinks ___ coffee___
_____ Sleep # hours _____
Snack: _____ Vitamins Yes ☐ No ☐

Discretionary Calories:
Fast food ☐☐☐☐☐ Sweets ☐☐☐☐☐
Junk food ☐☐☐☐☐ Other ☐☐☐☐☐

Every little bit of exercise counts!
Don't use the excuse that you don't have time!
You can fit in fitness all day long!
While you study sit on a fitness ball and work your abs!
Take a study break to walk or do some calisthenics.
Write your notes on index cards and walk while you study. Be creative and have fun!
Exercise will also help your stress level!

Week #8

> "Feeling grateful or appreciative of someone or something in your life actually attracts more of the things that you appreciate and value into your life."   Christiane Northrup

Name_____

Strength Training Log

Exercises	Date	Date	Exercises	Date	Date
Chest			Arms		
Back			Core		
Shoulders			Legs/Glutes		

Cardio Log

	Cardio	#	Intensity	#
	Exercise	Mins	Level	Miles
Mon				
Tue				
Wed				
Thur				
Fri				
Sat				
Sun				
	Total		Total	
	Minutes	____	Miles	____

Nutrition Goal for this week:

_____

Exercise Goal for this week:

© 2009 Betty Kern. Please don't make illegal copies of this page

	Monday	Tuesday	Wednesday	Thursday	Friday	Saturday	Sunday	Weekly Total	Challenge Total
Ab Exercises									
Push-ups									

Week 9

Name_____

Think about what you ate each day. Check off the boxes that apply to your intake. Did you meet your food group requirements? Remember to fill in your exercise chart on the back of this page!

	Monday	Tuesday	Wednesday	Thursday	Friday	Saturday	Sunday
Water	☐☐☐☐ ☐☐☐☐	☐☐☐☐ ☐☐☐☐	☐☐☐☐ ☐☐☐☐	☐☐☐☐ ☐☐☐☐	☐☐☐☐ ☐☐☐☐	☐☐☐☐ ☐☐☐☐	☐☐☐☐ ☐☐☐☐
Grains	☐☐☐☐☐☐	☐☐☐☐☐☐	☐☐☐☐☐☐	☐☐☐☐☐☐	☐☐☐☐☐☐	☐☐☐☐☐☐	☐☐☐☐☐☐
Fruit	☐☐☐☐☐	☐☐☐☐☐	☐☐☐☐☐	☐☐☐☐☐	☐☐☐☐☐	☐☐☐☐☐	☐☐☐☐☐
Veggies	☐☐☐☐☐	☐☐☐☐☐	☐☐☐☐☐	☐☐☐☐☐	☐☐☐☐☐	☐☐☐☐☐	☐☐☐☐☐
Meat/Beans	☐☐☐☐	☐☐☐☐	☐☐☐☐	☐☐☐☐	☐☐☐☐	☐☐☐☐	☐☐☐☐
Dairy	☐☐☐☐☐	☐☐☐☐☐	☐☐☐☐☐	☐☐☐☐☐	☐☐☐☐☐	☐☐☐☐☐	☐☐☐☐☐
Coffee/Soft Drinks	☐☐☐☐	☐☐☐☐	☐☐☐☐	☐☐☐☐	☐☐☐☐	☐☐☐☐	☐☐☐☐
Discretionary Calories	☐☐☐☐☐	☐☐☐☐☐	☐☐☐☐☐	☐☐☐☐☐	☐☐☐☐☐	☐☐☐☐☐	☐☐☐☐☐
Vitamins	Yes ☐ No ☐	Yes ☐ No ☐	Yes ☐ No ☐	Yes ☐ No ☐	Yes ☐ No ☐	Yes ☐ No ☐	Yes ☐ No ☐
Minerals	Yes ☐ No ☐	Yes ☐ No ☐	Yes ☐ No ☐	Yes ☐ No ☐	Yes ☐ No ☐	Yes ☐ No ☐	Yes ☐ No ☐
Breakfast	Yes ☐ No ☐	Yes ☐ No ☐	Yes ☐ No ☐	Yes ☐ No ☐	Yes ☐ No ☐	Yes ☐ No ☐	Yes ☐ No ☐
Sleep	# hours ____	# hours ____	# hours ____	# hours ____	# hours ____	# hours ____	# hours ____
Nutrition goal...	Yes ☐ No ☐	Yes ☐ No ☐	Yes ☐ No ☐	Yes ☐ No ☐	Yes ☐ No ☐	Yes ☐ No ☐	Yes ☐ No ☐
Exercise goal...	Yes ☐ No ☐	Yes ☐ No ☐	Yes ☐ No ☐	Yes ☐ No ☐	Yes ☐ No ☐	Yes ☐ No ☐	Yes ☐ No ☐
Sleep goal...	Yes ☐ No ☐	Yes ☐ No ☐	Yes ☐ No ☐	Yes ☐ No ☐	Yes ☐ No ☐	Yes ☐ No ☐	Yes ☐ No ☐
Study goal...	Yes ☐ No ☐	Yes ☐ No ☐	Yes ☐ No ☐	Yes ☐ No ☐	Yes ☐ No ☐	Yes ☐ No ☐	Yes ☐ No ☐
Attitude goal...	Yes ☐ No ☐	Yes ☐ No ☐	Yes ☐ No ☐	Yes ☐ No ☐	Yes ☐ No ☐	Yes ☐ No ☐	Yes ☐ No ☐

© 2009 Betty Kern. Please don't make illegal copies of this page

Take a minute to think about your relationships. Is there something you could do to improve your relationship with your parents or siblings? List one positive action you could do today that would improve your family relationships!

Week #9

> "Our self-talk, the thoughts we communicate to ourselves, in turn controls the way we feel and act." John Lembo

Name_____

Strength Training Log   Cardio Log

Exercises	Date	Date	Exercises	Date	Date
Chest			Arms		
Back			Core		
Shoulders			Legs/Glutes		

	Cardio	#	Intensity	#
	Exercise	Mins	Level	Miles
Mon				
Tue				
Wed				
Thur				
Fri				
Sat				
Sun				
	Total		Total	
	Minutes	____	Miles	____

Nutrition Goal for this week:

_____

Exercise Goal for this week:

© 2009 Betty Kern. Please don't make illegal copies of this page

	Monday	Tuesday	Wednesday	Thursday	Friday	Saturday	Sunday	Weekly Total	Challenge Total
Ab Exercises									
Push-ups									

Week 10

Monday water ☐☐☐☐☐☐☐☐☐
Breakfast: _____ dairy ☐☐☐☐☐☐
_____ veggies ☐☐☐☐☐☐
Lunch: _____ fruit ☐☐☐☐☐☐
_____ protein ☐☐☐☐
Snack: _____ carbs ☐☐☐☐☐☐
Dinner: _____ healthy fats ☐☐☐☐
_____ soft drinks ___ coffee __
_____ Sleep # hours _____
Snack: _____ Vitamins Yes ☐   No ☐

Discretionary Calories:
   Fast food ☐☐☐☐☐   Sweets ☐☐☐☐☐
   Junk food ☐☐☐☐☐   Other ☐☐☐☐☐

Tuesday water ☐☐☐☐☐☐☐☐☐
Breakfast: _____ dairy ☐☐☐☐☐☐
_____ veggies ☐☐☐☐☐☐
Lunch: _____ fruit ☐☐☐☐☐☐
_____ protein ☐☐☐☐
Snack: _____ carbs ☐☐☐☐☐☐
Dinner: _____ healthy fats ☐☐☐☐
_____ soft drinks ___ coffee __
_____ Sleep # hours _____
Snack: _____ Vitamins Yes ☐   No ☐

Discretionary Calories:
   Fast food ☐☐☐☐☐   Sweets ☐☐☐☐☐
   Junk food ☐☐☐☐☐   Other ☐☐☐☐☐

FITNESS TESTING RESULTS

Test	
Height	
Weight	
BMI	
% Body Fat	
Resting Heart Rate	
Aerobic Test	
Waist Circumference	

Wednesday water ☐☐☐☐☐☐☐☐☐
Breakfast: _____ dairy ☐☐☐☐☐☐
_____ veggies ☐☐☐☐☐
Lunch: _____ fruit ☐☐☐☐☐☐
_____ protein ☐☐☐☐
Snack: _____ carbs ☐☐☐☐☐☐
Dinner: _____ healthy fats ☐☐☐☐
_____ soft drinks ___ coffee __
_____ Sleep # hours _____
Snack: _____ Vitamins Yes ☐   No ☐

Discretionary Calories:
   Fast food ☐☐☐☐☐   Sweets ☐☐☐☐☐
   Junk food ☐☐☐☐☐   Other ☐☐☐☐☐

Thursday water ☐☐☐☐☐☐☐☐☐
Breakfast: _____ dairy ☐☐☐☐☐☐
_____ veggies ☐☐☐☐☐
Lunch: _____ fruit ☐☐☐☐☐☐
_____ protein ☐☐☐☐
Snack: _____ carbs ☐☐☐☐☐☐
Dinner: _____ healthy fats ☐☐☐☐
_____ soft drinks ___ coffee __
_____ Sleep # hours _____
Snack: _____ Vitamins Yes ☐   No ☐

Discretionary Calories:
   Fast food ☐☐☐☐☐   Sweets ☐☐☐☐☐
   Junk food ☐☐☐☐☐   Other ☐☐☐☐☐

Friday water ☐☐☐☐☐☐☐☐☐
Breakfast: _____ dairy ☐☐☐☐
_____ veggies ☐☐☐☐
Lunch: _____ fruit ☐☐☐☐☐☐
_____ protein ☐☐☐☐
Snack: _____ carbs ☐☐☐☐☐☐
Dinner: _____ healthy fats ☐☐☐☐
_____ soft drinks ___ coffee __
_____ Sleep # hours _____
Snack: _____ Vitamins Yes ☐   No ☐

Discretionary Calories:
   Fast food ☐☐☐☐☐   Sweets ☐☐☐☐☐
   Junk food ☐☐☐☐☐   Other ☐☐☐☐☐

Believe you can and you are half way there!

Saturday water ☐☐☐☐☐☐☐☐☐
Breakfast: _____ dairy ☐☐☐☐☐
_____ veggies ☐☐☐☐☐
Lunch: _____ fruit ☐☐☐☐☐☐
_____ protein ☐☐☐☐☐
Snack: _____ carbs ☐☐☐☐☐☐
Dinner: _____ healthy fats ☐☐☐
_____ soft drinks ___ coffee __
_____ Sleep # hours _____
Snack: _____ Vitamins Yes ☐   No ☐

Discretionary Calories:
   Fast food ☐☐☐☐☐   Sweets ☐☐☐☐☐
   Junk food ☐☐☐☐☐   Other ☐☐☐☐☐

Sunday water ☐☐☐☐☐☐☐☐☐
Breakfast: _____ dairy ☐☐☐☐☐☐
_____ veggies ☐☐☐☐☐
Lunch: _____ fruit ☐☐☐☐☐☐
_____ protein ☐☐☐☐☐
Snack: _____ carbs ☐☐☐☐☐☐
Dinner: _____ healthy fats ☐☐☐☐
_____ soft drinks ___ coffee __
_____ Sleep # hours _____
Snack: _____ Vitamins Yes ☐   No ☐

Discretionary Calories:
   Fast food ☐☐☐☐☐   Sweets ☐☐☐☐☐
   Junk food ☐☐☐☐☐   Other ☐☐☐☐☐

Congratulations on the work you have done this semester! You have made positive steps toward a healthier lifestyle!

Consistent habits are the secret to living a healthier life!

Never underestimate your ability to achieve your goals!

Week #10

Motivation is what gets you started; habit is what keeps you going! Keep following those healthy habits!

Name_____

Strength Training Log   Cardio Log

Exercises	Date	Date	Exercises	Date	Date
Chest			Arms		
Back			Core		
Shoulders			Legs/Glutes		

	Cardio	#	Intensity	#
	Exercise	Mins	Level	Miles
Mon				
Tue				
Wed				
Thur				
Fri				
Sat				
Sun				
	Total		Total	
	Minutes	____	Miles	____

Nutrition Goal for this week:

_____

Exercise Goal for this week:

© 2009 Betty Kern. Please don't make illegal copies of this page

Did you meet your challenge goals?

	Monday	Tuesday	Wednesday	Thursday	Friday	Saturday	Sunday	Weekly Total	Challenge Total
Ab Exercises									
Push-ups									

Workouts

Ball & Band Exercises

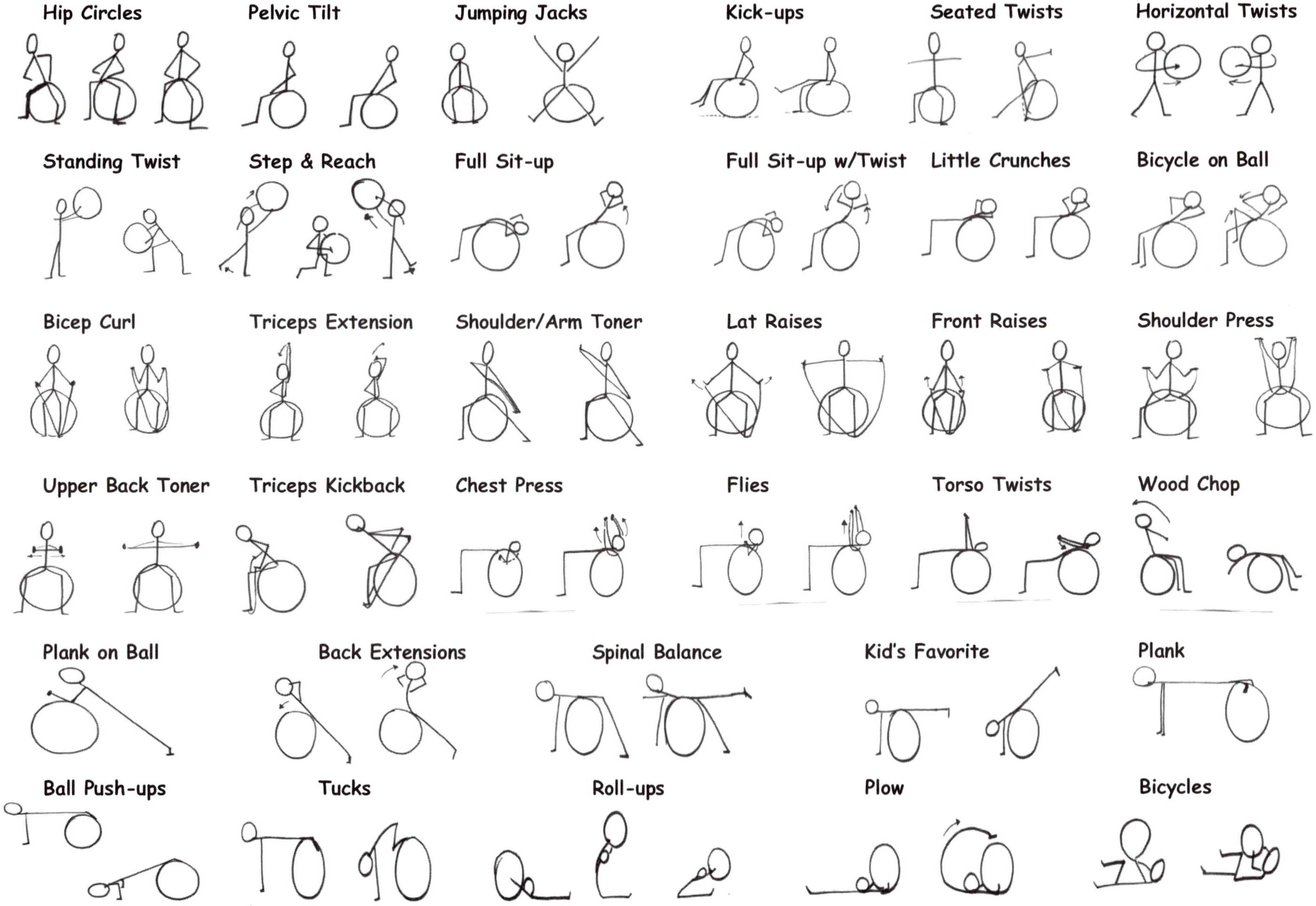

Hip Circles	Pelvic Tilt	Jumping Jacks	Kick-ups	Seated Twists	Horizontal Twists

Standing Twist	Step & Reach	Full Sit-up	Full Sit-up w/Twist	Little Crunches	Bicycle on Ball

Bicep Curl	Triceps Extension	Shoulder/Arm Toner	Lat Raises	Front Raises	Shoulder Press

Upper Back Toner	Triceps Kickback	Chest Press	Flies	Torso Twists	Wood Chop

Plank on Ball	Back Extensions	Spinal Balance	Kid's Favorite	Plank

Ball Push-ups	Tucks	Roll-ups	Plow	Bicycles

Hip Raises	Hamstring Curl	Bridge w/leg Raised	HS Curl w/leg Raised	Lower Ab Trimmer
Wall Squats	Balancing Deadlift	Glute Burner	Push-up on Ball	Squats w/ball Lift
Twisting Lunge	Balancing Lunge	Kneeling Leg Lift	Leg Lift	Dancer's Pose
Lower Ab Firmer	Roll-up 2	Teaser	Ab Burner	Warrior II
Triangle	Mermaid	Hamstring Stretch	Rainbow	Back Stretch & Relax
Cobra	Tripod		Child's Pose	Forward Stretch

Pilates & Yoga

Joseph Pilates developed the Pilates exercises in Germany, in the 1920s. His fitness program evolved though his life experiences. Initially, he studied different types of exercise to improve his health after a sickly childhood. Another experience involved working as a nurse during World War I where he began to rehabilitate internees with exercises he devised using improvised equipment. Later he assisted dancers, gymnasts, athletes and actors to rehabilitate injuries, improve muscular strength, posture, balance and gracefulness. After immigrating to the USA in the 1940s and establishing a fitness studio in New York City, his work continued to grow in popularity and effectiveness. Pilates' original 34 moves have evolved and grown throughout the years and are still considered an effective training method. Joseph Pilates intended for his routines to be a part of a program to improve a person's overall fitness and health. Pilates is meant to enhance current fitness programs not replace them. The routines augment fitness programs because they strengthen, re-align and rebalance the body, improve body awareness and reduce the risk of injury and strain. However, if an individual is not involved in a fitness program, Pilates can be a great place to start. Pilates offers a safe, non-jarring, easy on the joints, total body workout that can be adapted for all ages and fitness levels.

"Rehabilitates an injured body, strengthens a healthy one."
Joseph Pilates
Pilates believed that injuries were caused by imbalances in the body and habitual patterns of movement.
He observed that the body overcompensated for weaknesses in one area by recruiting other areas to support the imbalance.
Therefore, he designed his exercises to strengthen weak areas and to re-educate and re-align the body.

"Pilates works your body as a unit. Starting with your core and lengthening upward and outward."
Denise Austin

Benefits of Pilates

- Improves core abdominal strength
- Develops flatter, slimmer "abs"
- Develops lean muscle tone...look slimmer
- Improves balance, stability, flexibility, co-ordination
- Improves posture → reduce tension, headaches, backaches
  → look taller and slimmer
- Improves mental outlook, self-confidence and motivation
- Helps manage or reduce stress and fatigue → sleep better
- Reduces pain and tension
- Works the deep muscles of the body to build strength and control
- Enhances mind/body awareness → more in-tune with the needs of your body
- Improves muscle control
- Improves athletic performance
- Makes everyday activities easier
- Increases strength and tones without bulk
- Increases circulation and reduces tension
- Rehabilitates injuries
- Works into daily routine without any special equipment needed!

Pilates & Yoga Exercise Environment
Setting the Stage for Success

- Find a comfortable, quiet area
- Turn off cell phone, TV, computer, etc.
- Use a good, non-slip exercise mat
- Wear comfortable clothes but not baggy clothes
- Play soft, relaxing or soothing music
- Plan to exercise before meals or 2 hours after a meal
- Snack on fruit if needed prior to a session
- Begin session well-hydrated
- Keep water near to use during session
- Practice Pilates barefoot
- Be aware of your body's needs
- Listen to your body
- Work at your own pace

"Powerhouse"

Core/Abdominal Muscles

Four Muscles – work together to build a strong core which improves balance, flexibility, stability, flexibility and athletic performance. Plus, they help you look great!

1. **Rectus Abdonimis (6-pack)**
   - Runs from the sternum (breast bone) to the pubic bone
   - Maintains posture
   - Flexes body forward
   - Weak spot at the bottom of the muscle below the navel

2. **Internal Oblique**
   - Forms waist
   - Rotates the body
   - Flexes the body laterally (picking up a suitcase from the side)

3. **External Oblique**
   - Same as Internal Oblique

4. **Transverse Abdominis**
   - Key to a strong back (supports back)
   - Key to good posture
   - Key to a flat belly (holds in belly)
   - Wraps around the body

Key Elements of Pilates & Yoga

- Keep you safe and comfortable
- Become automatic over time and you may find yourself applying them to other activities

Breathing
- NEVER HOLD YOUR BREATH!
- Control breathing to stay focused and relaxed
- Don't let the ribs push upwards or outwards from the spine
- Aim to keep the ribs the same distance from the hips
- Breath laterally…sliding out to the sides and back

Concentration/Focus
- Focus on the work you expect the body to perform
- Control movements carefully through concentration
- Encourages the mind/body connection

Relaxation
- Relax muscles that are not used to perform the exercise
- Watch for tension in the jaw, face, neck and shoulders

Flow
- "Link" movements together
- Smooth
- Even paced and timed with breathing

Centering
- Focus on the "Powerhouse" (2 inches below navel)
- Move from core to keep spine and neck safe

Precision
- Execute movements precisely for maximum effectiveness
- Employ patience, practice and concentration

Adherence/Routine
- Practice regularly…Just does it!
- Make it part of your daily habits

Intuition/Integration
- Pilates will teach you to listen to your body
- Pay attention to how your body feels

Yoga

Benefits:

- Relaxation
- Increases Flexibility
- Increases Respiration
- Increases Circulation
- Improves Muscle Tone

- Improves Core Strength
- Improves Balance
- Improves ability to Focus
- Self-Awareness

In general, practicing yoga on a regular basis is the key to getting benefits of the practice. Setting aside 15-30 minutes a session is an adequate amount of time for beginners. You will want to wait at least four hours after a heavy meal before practicing yoga.

Guidelines:

Breathe slowly and quietly through the nostrils. Never hold your breath when moving into, maintaining, or coming out of a pose. Holding your breath can put a strain on the heart. Move into each pose with full awareness. Do not bounce or jerk into a stretch. This will cause the muscle to involuntarily contract and may cause injury. Go as far as you can into the stretch (pose) while maintaining a correct alignment. Maintain correct alignment for safety and effectiveness rather than sacrificing the pose so that you appear to be stretching further. When you are in a pose, you should feel tightness from stretching but never pain. Only work the muscles that are necessary to hold the pose. Relax any other muscles that may take an extra effort. For example, relax your eyes, face, shoulders, neck and any other muscles that are not necessary. When you need to adjust a pose, you should make these changes from the ground up. In standing poses, begin adjusting with feet. In a sitting pose, begin adjusting your buttocks and the placement of your pelvis. As with inverted poses (advanced), adjust your hands and work your way up. **When practicing yoga you should always go at your own pace. Never compete with the person next to you or with persons in a book, magazine, video or even the instructor.** Everyone is different and your stretching capacity will change from day to day as you practice your poses. Always enter into the learning of yoga with an open mind. It is best to always use common sense when practicing your poses. If something does not seem right, do not do it! Proceed with caution and HAVE FUN!

Yoga Session 1: →

Sunflowers		Moonflowers	Lateral Flexion (R/L)	Inhale arms up	Swan Dive Down

→ Forward Fold — Reverse Swam Dive Up — Chair — Inhale arms up — Swan Dive Down — Forward Fold

→ Monkey — Forward Fold — Reverse Swam Dive Up — Chair — Inhale arms up — Swan Dive Down

→ Forward Fold — Lunge Back to R knee — Ext. Child's Pose Rock Forward/Back — Ext. Child's Pose Rock Forward/Back

Ext. Child's Pose — Push-up & Back to Child's Pose Several Times — Cobra — Ext. Child's Pose

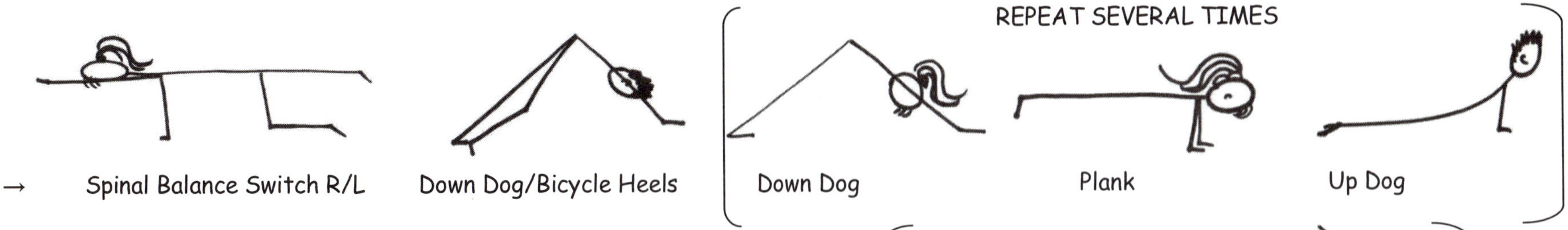

→ Spinal Balance Switch R/L

Down Dog/Bicycle Heels

REPEAT SEVERAL TIMES

Down Dog

Plank

Up Dog

→ Lunge Forward

SUN SALUTATION!
Repeat on both sides at least once!
See page 153

Warrior I

Warrior II

Reverse Warrior

REPEAT on OTHER SIDE!

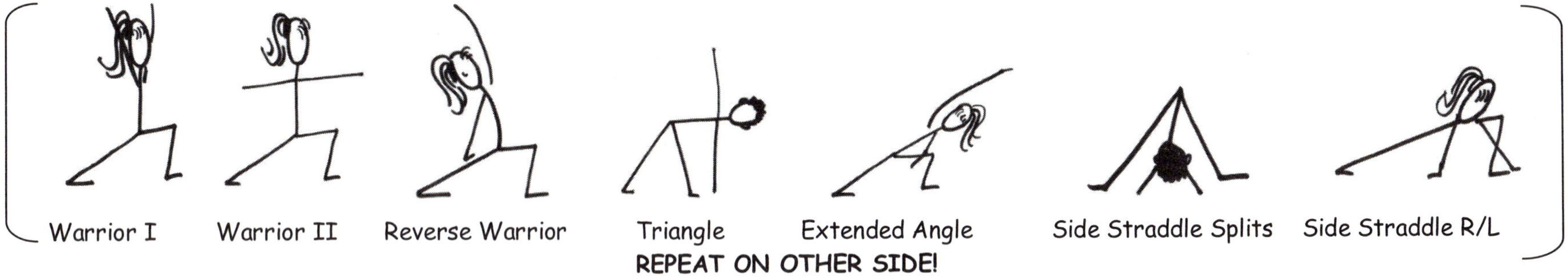

Warrior I

Warrior II

Reverse Warrior

Triangle

Extended Angle

Side Straddle Splits

Side Straddle R/L

REPEAT ON OTHER SIDE!

SKIP TO PAGE 154!

152

Sun Salutation – can be used as a general warm-up activity or as part of a yoga sequence.

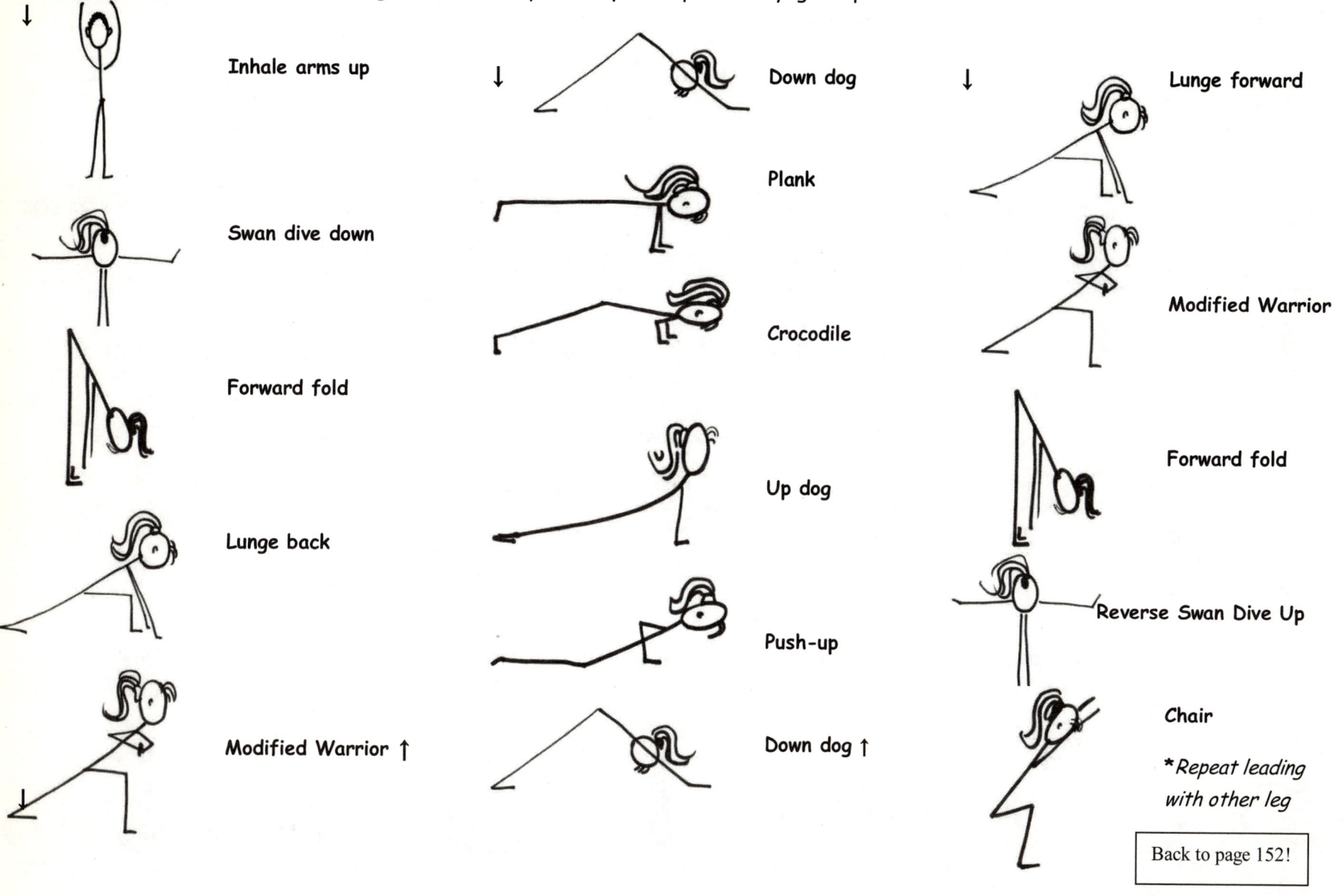

↓

Inhale arms up

Swan dive down

Forward fold

Lunge back

Modified Warrior ↑

↓

Down dog

Plank

Crocodile

Up dog

Push-up

Down dog ↑

↓

Lunge forward

Modified Warrior

Forward fold

Reverse Swan Dive Up

Chair

*Repeat leading with other leg

Back to page 152!

153

→ Tree Pose   Tree   Mountain   Inhale Arms Up   Swan Dive Down   Forward Fold   Lunge Back

→ Camel   Camel   Pigeon   Butterfly   Modified Boat   Boat   Leg Ext R/L

→ Both Legs   Cradle the Baby   Three-Leg Table Top   Twist look over shoulder R/L   Pigeon   REPEAT on OTHER SIDE!

→ Locust   Bow   Child's Pose   Knees to Chest R/L   Lying Spinal Twists R/L

→

Shoulder Stand   Plow   Fish   Bridge Sequence   Straight Leg Stretch R/L

DO NOT LOOK RIGHT OR LEFT...ONLY AT YOUR LEGS!

Knees to Chest R/L   Lying Spinal Twists R/L   Corpse Pose/RELAX!

SPEND A FEW MINUTES AT THE END IN QUIET RELAXATION...AS YOU EXHALE CHECK IN WITH YOUR BODY STARTING AT YOUR HEAD AND WORKING YOUR WAY DOWN...MAKING SURE YOUR MUSCLES ARE RELAXED AND NOT HOLDING TENSION. WHEN YOU ARE FINISHED WITH YOUR RELAXATION...ROLL ON TO YOUR SIDE FOR A FEW DEEP BREATHES BEFORE SITTING UP.

"Slimming Down Workout"

Goal: To improve muscle tone and slim down!
It would be beneficial to include some aerobic exercise also!

Strength Workout: 3 sets of 15-20 reps of each exercise
NO REST BETWEEN SETS...ALTERNATE EXERCISES!

1a. Lateral Raises

1b. Front Raises

1c. Shoulder Shrugs

1d. Shoulder Press

2a. Triceps Extensions

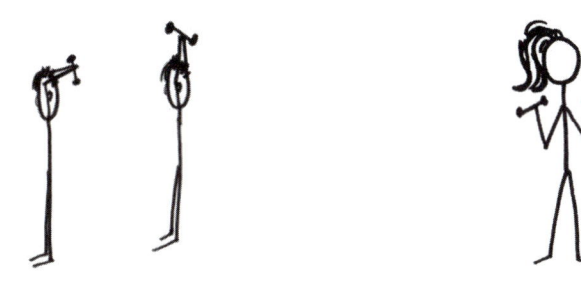

2b. Biceps Curl

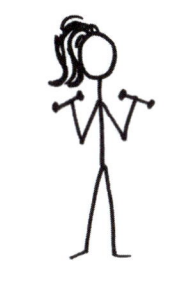

3a. Leg Extensions

3b. Leg Curls

4a. Ab Exercises...your choice

5a. Lunges & Squats

Perform exercises in groups according to the numbers without any rest between those sets then move on to the next group.
Once you can do 20 reps of any exercise, move on to a heavier weight.

Aerobic & Fitness Workout

Goals: Improve aerobic fitness and tome muscles!

A) **Aerobic Exercise:** run or walk on the treadmill or outside or use an elliptical or bike for 15 minutes.

B) **Strength Workout:** 2-3 sets of 12-15 reps of each exercise

1a. Leg Extensions

1b. Leg Curls

2a. Shoulder Press

2b. Lunges

3a. Tricep Extensions

3b. Ab Exercise

4a. Biceps Curl

4b. Back Extensions

5a. Squats

5b. Shoulder/Arm Toner

6a. Ball Push-ups

6b. Ball Tucks

Perform exercises in groups of two by alternating the a & b with no rest between them.
Then move on to the next set. This allows for more work to be accomplished in less time!
Notice that we are alternating upper body with lower body exercises, which allows for some recovery to occur.

"Muscle Building Workout"
Goals: To build muscle and gain strength!

Strength Workout: 3 sets of 6-8 reps of each exercise
The last few reps of each set should be very hard!
IN ORDER TO CONTINUE MAKING PROGRESS, YOU MUSTMOVE UP TO A HEAVIER WEIGHT
ONCE YOU CAN DO <u>8</u> REPS OF AN EXERCISE!

1. Bench Press - bar, db or band

2. Triceps Extensions

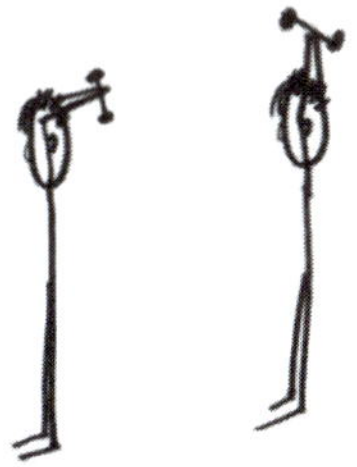

3. Biceps Curls

4. Shoulder Press

5. Leg Extensions

6. Leg Curls

7. Squats and or Lunges

8. Ab Exercises - your choice!

In order to make gains, you must rest between sets of these exercises. Rest at least 1 minute but not more than 2 minutes between sets. Work with a partner and alternate work and rest periods. If time is short, you could alternate between an upper body exercise and a lower body exercise or do ab exercises between sets of other exercises.

References
Information for this journal was derived from the following publications:

American Cancer Society. (2006) *The complete Guide – Nutrition & Physical Activity.* www.cancer.org.

American Cancer Society. (2007). *Skin Cancer Prevention and Early Detection.* www.cancer.org

American Cancer Society. (2007). *Recommended Health Screenings for People of Average Risk.* www.cancer.org

Applegate, L. Ph. D. (2001). *Eat Smart Play Hard.* Rodale Press.

ACSM Guideline for Exercise Testing & Prescription. 6th Edition, 2000.

Clark, N. (1991). *How to Gain Weight Healthfully.* The Physician & scportmedicine, 19, 9.

Delavier, F. (2003). *Women's Strength Training Anatomy.* Human Kinetics.

Demetre, D. (2003). *Scale Down.* Fleming H. Revell.

Fitness Resource Association, Inc. (2006). ACSM Workshop Study Guide.

Frediani, P. (2003). *Power Sculpt for Women.* Healthy Living Books.

Kelly, C. & London, S. (2005). *Dress Your Best.* Three Rivers press.

Kirberger, K. (2003). *No Body's Perfect.* Scholastics Inc.

Larimore, W. & Flynt, S. (2005). *Super Sized Kids.* New York: Center Street.

Liebman, B. *How Extra Pounds Boost Your Cancer Risk.* Nutrition Action Healthletter, September, 2007.

March of Dimes. *Pregnancy Articles.* www.marchofdimes.org.

McGraw, J. (2003). *The Ultimate Weight Solution for Teens.* New York: Free Press.

Muirhead, M. (2003). Total Pilates. MQ Publications Limited.

National Dairy Council. (1994). *How to Gain Weight.*

Northwest Health Sciences University (2007). www.nwhealth.edu

Platkin, C. S. (2005) *Lighten Up.* RAZORBILL.

Ruizen, M. MD, & Oz, M. MD. (2006) *You: The Owner's Manual.* Harper Collins.

Schlosser, E. & Monks, J. (2007). *Chew On This.* Houghton Mifflin Books.

Smith, J., Kelly, E, Monks, J. (2007). *Pilates & Yoga.* Barnes & Noble.

Young, L. PhD, RD. (2005). *The Portion Teller.* Morgan Road Books.